Government Printing Office

Translation of the General Law of Public Works of the Island

of Cuba,

and Regulations for its Execution...

Government Printing Office

Translation of the General Law of Public Works of the Island of Cuba,
and Regulations for its Execution...

ISBN/EAN: 9783744681124

Printed in Europe, USA, Canada, Australia, Japan

Cover: Foto ©Suzi / pixelio.de

More available books at **www.hansebooks.com**

TRANSLATION

OF THE

GENERAL LAW OF PUBLIC WORKS

OF THE

ISLAND OF CUBA,

AND

REGULATIONS FOR ITS EXECUTION.

WITH THE ADDITION OF ALL SUBSEQUENT PROVISIONS PUBLISHED TO DATE.

(1891.)

WAR DEPARTMENT,
DIVISION OF CUSTOMS AND INSULAR AFFAIRS.
1899.

WASHINGTON:
GOVERNMENT PRINTING OFFICE.
1899.

The Colonial Department, under date of the 19th of last April, communicates to His Excellency, the Governor-General, the following Royal Order:

Considering the reasons submitted to me by the Colonial Secretary, and by virtue of the authorization granted to the Government by Article 89 of the Constitution of the Monarchy, and in conformity with the report of the full Council of State, I have decreed as follows:

ARTICLE 1. In Cuba there shall govern a General Law of Public Works similar to that decreed for the Peninsula on the 13th of April, 1877.

ART. 2. The Colonial Secretary shall draft the regulations for the execution of this law and shall report this decree to the Cortes, which is sent to Your Excellency by Royal Order, accompanying the law with a copy of the Gaceta of Madrid, in which it has been published.

And in compliance with the superior order of Your Excellency, dated the 19th of the present month, it is published, together with said law, for general knowledge, together with the said General Law which extends it to this Island.

Havana, May 30, 1883.

M. DIAZ DE LA QUINTANA,
Secretary of the General Government.

3

GENERAL LAW OF PUBLIC WORKS FOR THE ISLAND OF CUBA.

[Approved by Royal Decree of this date.]

CHAPTER I.

CLASSIFICATION OF THE WORKS.

ART. 1. Public works for the purposes of this law shall be understood to be those which are of general use or service, and such constructions as are devoted to the service and are in charge of the State, of the Provinces, and of the towns.

In the first group are included roads, ordinary as well as railroads, ports, light-houses, great irrigation canals, navigation canals, and the works necessary to the disposition, use, and police of waters, retention of rivers within their beds, draining of lakes and marshes, and sanitation of lands. And the second group shall include public buildings devoted to service depending on the Colonial Department.

ART. 2. The examination and approval of the projects, supervision of the construction, and preservation of the public works, their police and use, shall always be dependent on the Administration, in whichsoever of its central powers, and on the provincial and municipal Administrations.

ART. 3. Public works, both in relation to their plans and their construction, operation, and preservation, may be charged to the State, to the Province, to Municipalities, or to individuals or companies.

ART. 4. There are in charge of the State:

First. The highroads which are included in the general plan of those which have to be taken care of with general funds.

Second. The work of retaining within their beds and making navigable the principal rivers.

Third. Ports of commerce of general interest, as well as those of refuge, and military ports.

Fourth. Light-houses and buoys.

Fifth. The drainage of great marshes, lakes, and inlets belonging to the State.

Sixth. The construction, preservation, and operation of those railroads of great national interest, which, because of high considerations of government, shall not be turned over to individuals or companies.

Seventh. All other railroads of general interest, in so far as concerns the concession, examination and approval of plans, and superindend-

5

ence, in order to see that they are constructed and operated in the safest and most proper manner.

Eighth. The construction and preservation of civil buildings necessary to the service of the Administration.

(Article 1 of the Regulations.)

ART. 5. There are in charge of the Province:

First. The roads included in the plan of those which have to be attended to with provincial funds.

Second. The ports within its territory which, not being included in the third paragraph of Article 4, offer greater advantages than those of a given locality.

Third. The sanitation of lakes, marshes, and inundated lands in which the Province is interested and which are not included in the fifth paragraph of said article 4.

Fourth. The construction and preservation of the buildings necessary for the service of the Provincial Administration.

(Article 56 of the Regulations.)

ART. 6. There are in charge of the Municipalities:

First. The construction and preservation of local roads included in the plan of those which have to be taken care of with municipal funds.

Second. The works for supplying water to the towns.

Third. The drainage of lakes and unhealthy lands which are not included in the fifth paragraph of Article 4, nor in the third paragraph of Article 5, and which affect one or more towns.

Fourth. Ports of merely local interest.

Fifth. The construction and preservation of the buildings necessary for the service of the municipal Administration.

Sixth. The works necessary to make and ornament the streets, squares, and boulevards of the towns.

(Article 91 of the Regulations.)

ART. 7. The following may be in charge of individuals or companies, in accordance with the general provisions of this law and the special provisions for each class of works:

First. Highroads and railroads in general.

Second. Ports.

Third. Irrigation and navigation canals.

Fourth. Drainage of lakes and marshes.

Fifth. Sanitation of unhealthy lands.

Sixth. Water supply of towns.

CHAPTER II.

ADMINISTRATION AND ECONOMIC MANAGEMENT OF PUBLIC WORKS.

ART. 8. The following shall be in charge of the Colonial Secretary:

First. All that refers to the plans, construction, preservation, repair, and police of the highroads in charge of the State.

Second. All that concerns the method and form of the constitution of partnerships or companies which may demand concessions of railroads of general interest, the granting of these concessions and privileges corresponding thereto, the examination and approval of the plans, and the service for the inspection which the State shall exercise in the construction, preservation, operation, and police of said railroads.

Third. All that refers to the construction and operation of those railroads of great public interest which, according to paragraph 6 of Article 4, are declared by special laws to be in charge of the State.

Fourth. Irrigation and navigation canals which may also be in charge of the State, in whatever relates to the drafting of plans, to works of construction, preservation, and improvement, and, finally, to the technical part of the distribution of the water and the policing of the navigation.

Fifth. The management and police of public waters, of rivers, torrents, lakes, streams, canals of artificial currents; the works relative to navigation, river navigation, to the defenses of the border of the rivers and lowlands exposed to be swept away or inundated; the draining of public waters, sanitation of marshy lands, and, finally, the technical policing of inland navigation.

Sixth. The works of construction, preservation, and repair of the ports in charge of the State, and the technical policing of the same.

Seventh. The light-houses and all classes of maritime signals and buoys on the coasts.

Eighth. Everything in connection with the construction, building of additions, improvement and preservation of the civil buildings devoted to services dependent on the Colonial Department, and with those constructions which have the character of artistic and historic monuments.

Ninth. The inspection of public works which are in charge of the Provinces or the Municipalities.

(Articles 78, 89, 101, and 120 of the Regulations.)

ART. 9. The Provincial Administration, according to the Organic Law, shall have charge of—

First. The highways, which, according to this Law, are in charge of the Provinces, as well as those which have to be provided for wholly with provincial funds in matters relative to the studies, construction, preservation, repair, and policing of said highroads.

Second. Navigation and irrigation canals declared to be exclusively of provincial interest, the technical part of the distribution of the water, and of the policing of the navigation.

Third. The sanitation of lakes and marshy lands declared of exclusive interest to the Provinces.

Fourth. The construction and improvement of the buildings having a provincial character devoted to public service, and the preservation of historic and artistic monuments.

(Article 56 of the Regulations.)

ART. 10. The Municipal Administration shall, in accordance with the Organic Laws, have charge of—

First. The construction, repair, and preservation of local roads paid for by the Municipal Councils or which should be in charge of them, according to the provisions of this Law.

Second. The water supply of towns, in so far as the construction of the works or the concession of the same to private enterprises is concerned.

Third. The drainage of lakes or unhealthy lands which are declared of purely local interest.

Fourth. The construction and preservation of ports of local interest.

Fifth. The construction and improvement of buildings devoted to public service which depend on the Colonial Department, and the preservation of historic and artistic monuments.

Sixth. Highways and ornamentation of towns.

(Article 91 of the Regulations.)

ART. 11. The public works which have to be paid for with funds of the State shall be executed subject to the credits voted in the general budgets or in special laws.

ART. 12. In all the annual or general budgets of the State there must appear exactly the amounts necessary for the preservation of actually existing public works, which are in charge of the Colonial Department, as well as those which the economic resources will permit for carrying on those already commenced, and for undertaking other new ones.

ART. 13. No amount whatever can be expended in public works of the State in this Island under the Colonial Department, except in accordance with a project duly approved, according to the provisions of the present law.

ART. 14. In the annual budgets of the Provinces, there must be included exactly the amounts which may be necessary for the preservation of such actually existing works as are in charge of the Provinces, as well as whatever the resources of the said Provinces may permit for the prosecution of those already begun and for the undertaking of other new ones.

(Article 64 of the Regulations.)

ART. 15. No other provincial public work can be undertaken except in accordance with a project previously approved by the proper Deputation, after report of the Chief Engineer of the Province, or of the Provincial Architect, if there be one, in case of a work included under the name of civil construction.

(Articles 59, 89, and 120 of the Regulations.)

ART. 16. In the municipal budgets there shall appear precisely the amounts necessary for the preservation of public works which are in charge of the Municipal Councils, as well as what the resources of the

Municipality may permit for the prosecution of those already commenced and for the undertaking of other new ones.

(Article 99 of the Regulations.)

ART. 17. No other municipal public work can be undertaken without a project previously approved by the Governor of the Province, after hearing the Chief Engineer of the same, or the Provincial or Municipal Architect, in case of a civil building or construction.

(Article 93 of the Regulations.)

ART. 18. In the execution of all public works there must be observed, in so far as the investment of general provincial or municipal funds is concerned, the rules established in the Law of Accounting and in the organic laws of the Deputation and the Municipal Councils of this Island, as well as in the provisions of the Royal Decree of the 5th of May, 1876, in force for contracting public works when they are to be executed by contract.

CHAPTER III.

WORKS PAID FOR BY THE STATE.

ART. 19. The Colonial Department shall, at the proper time, formulate the general plan of public works which have to be paid for by the State, presenting the respective drafts of the law, in which these are determined and classified in their order of preference, to the Cortes.

(Article 2 of the Regulations.)

ART. 20. The Government can not undertake any public work for which there has not been a provision made in the budgets, assigning the proper credit. In any other case, in order to undertake a work, it shall be necessary for the Government to be authorized to do so by a special law. From this requisite are excepted works of mere repair, as well as those of new construction, which shall be declared of admitted urgency by the Colonial Department or its delegates, after report of the Consulting Board of Roads, Canals, and Ports and of the full Council of State.

(Articles 9, 10, 11, and 12 of the Regulations.)

The Colonial Secretary shall himself make use of the privilege to declare a work of admitted urgency which this article confers on him, when its value exceeds five thousand pesos. If the amount should be less, the Governor-General may authorize its execution, after favorable report of the Chief Engineer of the Province and of the Administrative Council which hears disputes, immediately reporting it to the Government.

ART. 21. No amounts whatsoever shall be included in the general budgets of the State for public works which are not included in the plans referred to in Article 19, unless the Government has been authorized to do so by a special law. In any case, in order to include the value of a work in the general budget, it shall be necessary that there be a previous study made and that the project receive the proper approval.

Concerning works of preservation and repair, it shall be sufficient that the general credit for this purpose be included in the budgets of the State existing at the time in which these works are to be executed.

(Article 13 of the Regulations.)

ART. 22. With the legislative credits, the Government may order the study of public works, the execution of which it deems convenient, in compliance with the provisions of the two preceding articles.

(Articles 3, 4, 5, 6, 7, 8, 9, 10, 11, and 12 of the Regulations.)

ART. 23. The Government may impose assessments and taxes for the use of works which are building with general funds, without prejudice to the rights which may have been acquired, and making report thereof to the Cortes.

ART. 24. The Government may construct the works in charge of the State by management or by contract. The first method shall be applied only to those works which can not be contracted for because of their special conditions, or because they can not be easily provided for in the budgets, because of the predomination of the hazardous parts in them, or for any other reason.

(Article 14 of the Regulations.)

ART. 25. The Government may contract for public works of which it may be in charge:

First. By obligating itself to pay the value of the works, according as they are being constructed at the times, and in the manner which may be determined on in the special provisions of each contract, and in the general conditions which should be contained in all those referring to this service.

Second. By granting to contractors the right to dispose of, for a specified time, the proceeds of the assessments which may have been established for the use of the work according to the provisions of Article 23 of the present law.

Third. By combining the two methods referred to.

(Article 17 of the Regulations.)

ART. 26. When the works which the State has constructed may be operated with profit, this shall be done by means of a contract awarded after public bidding, excepting in the cases in which, because of special circumstances, it is declared proper that the Government shall take charge thereof. This declaration shall be made by a decree issued by the Colonial Department, after hearing the Consulting Board of Roads, Canals, and Ports, and the Colonial Department of the Council of State.

(Articles 6 and 54 of the Regulations.)

ART. 27. In the works which are executed at the expense of the State in the manner indicated in the second and third paragraphs of Article 25, the prices which are fixed for the use and operation of said works shall not exceed the schedule of rates in accordance with which the award may have been made; but these rates may be reduced if the person to whom the award has been made shall deem it convenient, subject to the conditions which are prescribed in the contract.

ART. 28. In the articles of conditions of each contract shall be included the gratuitous services which those to whom the contract has been awarded must render, and the special rates for different public services.

ART. 29. The study of the projects, the direction of the works which are executed by management, and the supervision of those which are constructed by contract, shall, in all cases where the works are in charge of the State, be carried on by the Corps of Engineers of Roads, Canals, and Ports. The Government, through the same Engineers, shall carry on the inspection of provincial and municipal works which, according to the ninth paragraph of Article 8 of the present Law, is attributed to it.

Civil constructions are excepted, the study, management, and supervision of which should be intrusted to architects having professional degrees, who shall be approved by the Colonial Secretary.

(Articles 15 and 18 of the Regulations.)

ART. 30. Contractors shall be at liberty to select such persons as they may deem proper for the direction of the works which they obligate themselves to construct, who shall in all cases exercise their duties under the surveillance and inspection of the Government agents, as provided for in the previous article.

ART. 31. Contractors of State works, their employees, and laborers shall have the local benefits of the use of firewood, pasturage, and other rights which the inhabitants of the towns within the district in which said works are included, may enjoy.

ART. 32. The works of preservation and repair which are necessary for works in charge of the State, shall be carried on by the Colonial Department, adjusting themselves to the credits which shall have been assigned for that purpose in the general budgets, in accordance with the provisions of Article 12 and of paragraph 2 of Article 21 of this Law.

(Article 8 of the Regulations.)

CHAPTER IV.

PROVINCIAL WORKS.

ART. 33. There shall be established in each Province, after the proceedings which the Regulations may provide, the plans of public works, which, in accordance with Article 5 of this Law, shall be in charge of the respective Deputation.

These plans, in which the works shall be classified, showing the order of preference in which they should be constructed, shall be submitted for the approval of the Colonial Secretary.

(Articles 56, 57, and 58 of the Regulations.)

ART. 34. No works shall be undertaken at the expense of provincial funds, unless there be included the proper credit for this purpose in the budget of expenses of the Province.

ART. 35. In order that the appropriation for a public provincial work be included in the general expenses of the Province, it shall be necessary that said work be included in one of the plans referred to in Article 33, and that its project be previously and duly approved in the manner prescribed by Article 15 of the present Law.

Exception is made, however, of cases of admitted urgency, in which, after a special law or declaration of the Colonial Secretary, and after the proceedings provided for by the Regulations have taken place, the necessary credit for the execution of the work in question may be included in the budget of the expenses of the Province. But even in these special cases the proceedings of the study of the project and its approval must always have been first had, in accordance with the provisions of said Article 15, and also the declaration of public utility, which should be made in accordance with the provisions of the present law.

(Articles 60, 62, and 63 of the Regulations.)

ART. 36. With the credits which shall be included in the provincial budget, the Deputations may decide that the study of such public works in their charge as they may deem proper, shall be made, in accordance with the provisions of the two preceding articles.

ART. 37. The Provincial Deputations may impose taxes for the use of the work in their charge in order to reimburse themselves for the amount which they may have devoted to that purpose. The imposition of these taxes shall in all cases be submitted for the approval of the Government.

(Articles 65 and 87 of the Regulations.)

ART. 38. The Deputations may execute their works by management or by contract, proceeding in each case as provided by Articles 24 to 28, both inclusive, of the present Law in the manner prescribed therein concerning the works in charge of the State.

(Articles 60 and 61 of the Regulations.)

ART. 39. The projects, direction, and supervision of the works which are executed with provincial funds, shall be carried on by Engineers of Roads or by Assistants of Public Works. Civil constructions of a provincial character are excepted, which may be in charge of architects who have their professional degree.

Among the conditions established in each case shall be the naming of these technical agents by the proper Provincial Deputation.

(Articles 61, 66, 67, 68, and 71 of the Regulations.)

ART. 40. Contractors of provincial works may submit the direction of the same to such persons as they may deem proper, keeping in mind the provisions of Article 30 concerning the works of the State; and these persons shall have the benefits allowed by Article 31 to those who contract for works which shall be executed with general funds.

ART. 41. The works of preservation and repair which may be neces-sary for the works which are in charge of the Provinces, shall be carried on with reference to the credits which, as provided in Article 14 of the present Law, shall appear in the provincial budgets.

(Article 64 of the Regulations.)

ART. 42. Provincial public works shall be inspected by the Govern-ment, in accordance with the provisions of this Law, whenever the Colonial Secretary or the Governor-General thus orders, which shall at least be when they are finished and before they are turned over to public use.

(Articles 69 and 70 of the Regulations.)

CHAPTER V.

MUNICIPAL WORKS.

ART. 43. Municipal Councils shall, by the proceedings prescribed by the Regulations, formulate the plans of public works which may be in their charge, which shall be submitted for the approval of the Gov-ernor of the Province. If, from the decision of said authority approv-ing or disapproving these plans there should be any appeal, the entire proceedings shall be sent to the Colonial Secretary, who shall defi-nitely decide.

(Articles 91 and 92 of the Regulations.)

ART. 44. No municipal work can be carried out if in the budget of the respective Municipal Council there shall not be a credit assigned for this purpose, in the manner prescribed by the Laws and Regu-lations.

(Article 93 of the Regulations.)

ART. 45. In order that the appropriation for a municipal work may appear in the budget of the proper Municipal Council, it is necessary that said work be included in one of the plans referred to in Article 43, and that its project shall have been duly approved in the manner pre-scribed by Article 17 of the present Law. Exception is made in cases of admitted urgency, when, after the Governor has declared it, and after the Provincial Deputation has been heard, and with the right of appeal to the Governor on the part of the Municipal Council interested, there may be included in the Municipal budget the credit necessary for the execution of the work. Even in such cases a plan must have pre-viously been drawn and the project approved, and the declaration of public utility of the works made, in conformity with the provisions of the present Law. For the approval of plans for municipal works affecting territories of towns belonging to different provinces, the Gov-ernors of the said provinces shall agree, and if there be any disagree-ment the papers shall be sent through the Governor-General with his report to the Colonial Secretary, who, after hearing the opinion of the

Consulting Board of Roads, Canals, and Ports, shall decide, with no further appeal.

(Articles 95 and 96 of the Regulations.)

ART. 46. Municipal Councils may impose assessments and taxes on the works which are executed at their cost in order to reimburse themselves for the amount which they may have expended. For the imposition of these taxes the authorization of the Government shall be necessary, which, in order to grant it, shall first hear the report of the Governor of the Province.

(Articles 98 and 119 of the Regulations.)

ART. 47. Municipal Councils may construct their works by management or by contract, subject to the provisions of the present Law concerning this matter, in connection with the works in charge of the State and of the Provinces.

(Article 94 of the Regulations.)

ART. 48. For the drafting of projects, direction and supervision of the works which have to be constructed with municipal funds, Municipal Councils may name the person whom they believe best fitted therefor, provided he has the necessary professional degree to accredit his ability.

(Articles 100 and 102 of the Regulations.)

ART. 49. The works of preservation and repair which are necessary for works in charge of Municipal Councils, shall be carried out without any other limitation than that they must come within the credits which, in accordance with Article 16, shall be contained in the municipal budgets for that purpose.

(Article 99 of the Regulations.)

ART. 50. Roads of communication, and the other public works which are constructed at the expense of the Municipal Councils, shall be inspected by the technical agents of the Government whenever the Governor may deem this proper, and in all cases shall be submitted to the inspection of these agents before being turned over to public use.

From this provision is excepted the ordinary building of paths and local roads.

(Articles 101 and 110 of the Regulations.)

CHAPTER VI.

WORKS EXECUTED BY INDIVIDUALS FOR WHICH NO SUBSIDY OR OCCUPATION OF THE PUBLIC DOMAIN IS ASKED.

(Articles 89, 90, and 120 of the Regulations.)

ART. 51. Individuals and companies may construct, without further restrictions than those imposed by the Police, Safety, and Public Health Regulations, any work whatsoever of private interest which does not occupy or affect the public domain or that of the State, or which does not demand the exercise of the right of eminent domain over private property.

ART. 52. Individuals and companies may also build and operate public works devoted to general use and the others which are enumerated in Article 7 of this Law, when given the right to do so by concession.

ART. 53. Said concessions, providing that no subsidy or constant occupation of the public domain is requested, or that they do not destroy the plans which are referred to in Articles 19, 33, and 43, shall be granted by the Colonial Department, by the Provincial Deputation, or by the Municipal Council, respectively, in whose charge the works may be. The concessions of works for which no subsidy is requested, but which destroy the plans of the works in charge of the State, referred to in Article 19, can not be granted except by means of a law. In the same case those which destroy the plans of municipal or provincial works, referred to in Articles 33 and 43, can not be granted except by means of Royal Decrees issued by the Colonial Department.

(Articles 19, 72, 73, 103, and 104 of the Regulations.)

ART. 54. In all cases the concessions referred to in the preceding article shall not be granted for more than ninety-nine years, unless the very character of the work should demand a longer period, which shall be always granted by a law. When the time of the concession has run, the work shall become the property of the State, of the Province, or of the Municipality in whose charge it might be. Every concession shall be granted without prejudice to third parties and protecting the interests of private persons.

ART. 55. In order that a concession to an individual or company of a work in the cases referred to in Article 53 may be granted, there shall be necessary a project with all the facts which, according to the provisions of the Regulations, may be necessary to form a judgment of the work, of its objects, and of the advantages which will inure to the general interests from its construction.

(Articles 20, 21, 22, 74, and 105 of the Regulations.)

ART. 56. In order to form the project referred to in the preceding article, the petitioner may request of the Colonial Department, of the Governor-General, or of the proper corporations, the necessary authorization.

This authorization shall only carry with it—

The power to enter the private property of another in order to make the studies, after having received the permission of the owner, manager, or attendant who may reside on the property or near it; and otherwise, or when this is not granted, on the permission of the Alcalde, who shall always grant it when there is security, by means of a reasonable sum, for the immediate payment of the damages which may arise.

(Articles 20, 21, 74, and 105 of the Regulations.)

ART. 57. Individuals or companies which ask to construct or operate a public work, shall direct their petition to the Colonial Secretary, to the Governor-General, or to the corporation which in each case has power to grant the concession, accompanied by the project mentioned in Article 55, and also by a document showing that there has been deposited, as a guaranty of the proposal, 1 per cent of the estimate of said work.

(Articles 23, 75, and 106 of the Regulations.)

ART. 58. The Government, in cases in which it has the right to do so in accordance with Article 53, shall grant the concession, after consulting, in order better to form its judgment, the reports which concern each kind of works which may be established by special laws and by the Regulations, there being necessary as an indispensable requisite for the approval of the project, the previous opinion of the Consulting Board of Roads, Canals, and Ports, or of the Royal Academy of San Fernando, as the case may be.

When, according to the provisions of said article, a concession has to be granted by the legislative power, the Colonial Secretary shall present to the Cortes the proper form of law, if from the proceedings there should result the approval of the convenience of carrying out the work referred to in the petition.

The Provincial Deputation and Municipal Councils shall follow the provisions of the Regulations for the course of the proceedings to obtain the concession which they may have power to grant, in accordance with Article 53 of the present Law.

(Articles 24, 25, 26, 27, 76, 77, 107, 108, and 109 of the Regulations.)

ART. 59.—As a general rule, there shall appear in the terms of every concession the following:

First. The amount which shall be deposited by the concessionaire as a guaranty of the fulfillment of his engagements, which shall be from 3 to 5 per cent of the estimate of the works.

Second. The time in which the work shall begin and end.

Third. The conditions for the establishment and for the use of the works, which in each case may be deemed convenient, in accordance with the laws.

Fourth. The cases of forfeiture and the consequences of this forfeiture.

(Articles 28, 29, 77, 109, and 110 of the Regulations.)

ART. 60. The asking of subsidy after the said concession has been granted, shall be considered as a case of forfeiture of a concession included in Article 53. When by means of a law a subsidy or an aid with public funds in order to execute the work shall be granted, the subsidy or the aid shall not inure directly to the benefit of the former concessionaire, but only to that of the work itself, which shall be immediately submitted to public auction, in accordance with the provisions of this Law, concerning subsidized works.

(Article 29 of the Regulations.)

ART. 61. When more than one petition for the same work is presented, the one shall be preferred which offers the greatest advantages to the public interests. In order to determine these advantages, the Colonial Department, or the corporations which in a proper case have the right to grant the concessions, shall proceed to obtain the reports provided for by the Regulations.

When the Colonial Secretary has the authority to grant the concession, before deciding on the preference between the petitions, he shall hear the corporation interested and the Colonial Department of the Council of State.

(Articles 33, 80, 112, 113, and 118 of the Regulations.)

ART. 62. If from the reports referred to in the preceding article it shall appear that there is an equality among the proposals made, the concession shall be granted by means of a public bidding, in which not only the petitioners, but any other person who shall prove that he has made the deposit of one per cent of the estimate of the work, may take part.

The bidding shall be in the first place on the reduction of the rates of operation, and if in these there should result an equality of reductions, then in the period of the concession. The one to whom the award is made shall be obliged to pay to the signer of the petition which may have been first presented, in case the latter shall not have been the best bidder, the expenses of the project according to the expert appraisal of the same made before the public bidding.

(Articles 34, 35, 36, 37, 38, 39, 81, 82, 113, and 114 of the Regulations.)

ART. 63. No concession of a public work, asked by companies or individuals, can be made without the previous publication of their petition in the Gaceta de Madrid and of Havana and in the Boletin Oficial of the respective province, fixing the period of thirty days for the admission of other propositions which may be better than the first.

(Article 32 of the Regulations.)

ART. 64. When the concession of a public work is made, the Government, or the corporations which in a proper case may have granted it, shall supervise, through their technical agents, the construction of the work, in order that the stipulated conditions may be observed. The same supervision shall be observed in connection with the operation, when the works have been completed, and when such operation is authorized in the manner prescribed by the Regulations.

(Articles 40, 78, and 110 of the Regulations.)

ART. 65. The concessionaire may, after authorization by the Colonial Department, or the corporation which may have granted the concession, alienate the works, provided that the grantee shall obligate himself in the same terms and with the same guaranties as the first concessionaire, for the fulfillment of the stipulated conditions.

ART. 66. The guaranty referred to in the first paragraph of Article 39 shall not be returned to the concessionaire until he has proved the construction of works to an amount equivalent to a third part of those included in the concession. Said works shall then take the place of the guaranty, and shall be liable for the fulfillment of the provisions of the concession.

(Article 28 of the Regulations.)

21634——2

ART. 67. The declaration of forfeiture of the concession of a public work of those included in this Chapter, whenever made, shall be by the Colonial Department, or the corporation which might have granted it, and always after proceedings in which the interested party must be heard.

(Articles 29, 30, 78, and 111 of the Regulations.)

ART. 68. The forfeiture of the concession by reason of infractions imputable to the concessionaire shall always carry with it the loss of the guaranty, to the benefit of the general Provincial or Municipal Administration, as the case may be.

(Articles 31, 79, and 111 of the Regulations.)

ART. 69. If on the declaration of forfeiture the construction of the work shall not even have been commenced, the Administration shall be relieved of all agreements with the concessionaire. If the works have already been commenced, but if they should not be sufficient in order to return his guaranty to the concessionaire, the works constructed shall be offered to public bidding for a period of three months, and the basis of the bids shall be the value of the acquired lands, of the completed works, or the materials thereon. The works shall be awarded to the one who offers most for them, and the new concessionaire shall then pay to the first the amount of the bid, and shall be subrogated to him in all his rights and obligations. In both cases the first concessionaire shall forfeit his guaranty.

(Articles 31, 79, and 111 of the Regulations.)

ART. 70. If on the declaration of forfeiture the guaranty shall have been returned, the works completed by the concessionaire shall in the same way be offered to public bidding, for a period of two months, on the same basis. From the amount offered by the best bidder, who shall be declared to be the owner of the concession, the Administration shall reserve the amount of the returned guaranty, and the difference, should there be any, shall be turned over to the first concessionaire.

(Articles 31, 79, and 111 of the Regulations.)

ART. 71. In the cases of the preceding articles, if there shall not be any auction by reason of an absence of bidders, the executed work shall again be put up for public bids for a period of one month, on the same basis.

If the concession is not awarded in any of the auctions, the State, Province, or towns which may have granted the execution of the works, shall take charge and shall use them in the manner deemed convenient, without the right to any claim whatsoever on the part of the concessionaire, whose rights shall be declared forfeited.

(Articles 31, 79, and 111 of the Regulations.)

ART. 72. No work for the operation of which there may be necessary the occupation of another work belonging to the State, the Province, or towns can be granted without previous public bidding, on the basis which may be determined for this purpose. There shall be reserved the right of preference on equal terms to the petitioner, and when the concession is not granted to him he shall be paid, by the one to whom it is awarded, the amount of the project, according to expert appraisal made and advertised before the public sale.

(Articles 38, 82, and 114 of the Regulations.)

CHAPTER VII.

WORKS SUBSIDIZED WITH PUBLIC FUNDS, BUT WHICH DO NOT OCCUPY THE PUBLIC DOMAIN.

(Articles 89, 90, and 120 of the Regulations.)

ART. 73. Whenever a subsidy of any kind is requested for the execution by individuals or companies of a public work, which shall not constantly occupy or make use of a part of the public domain, the concession for this purpose, when the subsidy shall be given by a Province or some Municipality, shall be made by the corporation in whose charge the works are, but in every case after public bidding; and if the subsidy shall come from the State the concession shall moreover be the subject of a law.

By subsidy, for the purposes of this article, is understood any direct or indirect aid whatsoever from the public funds, including the exemption of customs duties on the material which is to be introduced from abroad, which exemption must always be granted by a law.

(Articles 73 and 104 of the Regulations.)

ART. 74. The concessions referred to in the preceding article shall always be temporary and can not exceed ninety-nine years. When this period has elapsed, the work shall become the property of the State, Province, or town which may have granted the subsidy.

ART. 75. The individuals or companies who request a subsidy of public funds to construct a work of those referred to in this Chapter, may ask for the necessary authorization to make the proposed studies in the terms and with the rights mentioned in Article 56 of the present Law. The petition for the concession shall be accompanied by a complete project of the works, according to the provisions of the Regulations, and also a document showing that the petitioner has deposited, as a guaranty for the fulfillment of the propositions which he may have made or admitted in the course of the proceedings, the 1 per cent of the total estimate of the said works.

(Articles 41, 83, and 115 of the Regulations.)

ART. 76. The Colonial Department, or the proper corporation, shall make investigation, as determined by the Regulations, in order to prove the utility of the project. If the work referred to should be included in the plans referred to in Articles 19, 33, and 43 of this Law, it shall not be necessary to make this investigation.

(Articles 41, 83, and 115 of the Regulations.)

ART. 77. When the project is approved in the manner prescribed by the Regulations, when the work has been gone over on the ground by the Engineers of the State, or by the technical officials designated by the Deputation or Municipal Councils, according to circumstances, and when the conditions of the concession are mutually accepted, the Colonial Secretary, in case of State works, shall present to the Cortes the form of law necessary to grant it, in accordance with the provisions of Article 73.

(Articles 41, 42, 43, and 84 of the Regulations.)

ART. 78. When the maximum subsidy which may be given for the projected work has been fixed by a law, in case of State works, or by the Deputation or the proper Municipal Council, in case of works in charge of these corporations, the concession shall be offered for public bids on this basis for three months; and it shall be awarded to the best bidder, with the obligation to pay to the petitioner, if he should not be given the award, the value of the studies of the project, in accordance with the expert appraisal made and announced previously to the bidding, in the form determined by the Regulations.

(Articles 43, 44, 45, 52, 53, 84, 86, and 116 of the Regulations.)

ART. 79. In order to take part in the bidding it is necessary to prove that there has been deposited, as a guaranty of the propositions which are presented, the 1 per cent of the total value of the work, according to the approved estimate.

(Articles 43, 84, and 116 of the Regulations.)

ART. 80. In no case can the instrument awarding the concession be executed until the concessionaire has proved that he has deposited, as a guarantee of the fulfillment of his obligations, 5 per cent of the estimated value of the works.

If the concessionaire allows fifteen days to pass without depositing the guaranty, the award shall be declared to be without effect, with the loss of the deposit referred to in the preceding article, the concession or the work being again put up for public bids for the period of forty days.

The guaranty treated of in this article shall not be returned to the company to which the concession is granted until the works of the concession shall be completely finished and in condition for operation.

(Articles 46, 85, and 117 of the Regulations.)

ART. 81. The provisions of Article 64 of the present law concerning the supervision which the Administration must exercise over the works during their construction and operation, are applicable to subsidized works.

The supervision of subsidized works shall extend also to the economic and mercantile part of the company to which the concession is granted, so that the delivery of the aids or subsidies shall be made in proportion to the executed works, in accordance with the stipulated provisions.

(Articles 55 and 88 of the Regulations.)

ART. 82. No variation or modification whatever may be made in the project which shall serve as the basis of a subsidized concession without a competent authorization of the Colonial Department or the corporation which might have granted it.

The authorization of the Colonial Department in connection with works subsidized by the State can not be granted until after hearing the proper corporation and the full Council of State, and after fulfilling the other requisites required by the Regulations for the execution of this law.

(Articles 47 and 45 of the Regulations.)

ART. 83. When, in consequence of the variations referred to in the preceding article, the cost of the works is diminished, the amount of the aid or subsidy shall be reduced proportionately to such diminution.

If the variations or modifications should result in increasing the cost, even when by means of them the works will be perfected or advantages obtained in their use or operation, the subsidies and the aids granted by the law of concession shall not for these reasons be increased unless the contrary shall be provided for by special law.

(Articles 47 and 85 of the Regulations.)

ART. 84. The declaration of forfeiture of the subsidized concession shall be made by the Colonial Department in all cases affecting State works, and in the other cases by the Deputation or the Municipal Council which, in accordance with Article 73, may have granted such concessions.

Whenever the forfeiture of a concession with subsidy has been finally declared, the amount of the guaranty which, in accordance with Article 80, may have been required from the concessionaire, shall remain for the benefit of the State, or of the proper corporation.

(Articles 48 and 85 of the Regulations.)

ART. 85. Concessions of subsidized public works shall be absolutely forfeited if the work shall not be begun or terminated entirely, or in the parts into which it may have been divided, within the time determined on.

Whenever there is a case of force majeure, and it is duly proved by virtue of an investigation made, as provided by the Regulations, the time may be extended for that absolutely necessary. If the subsidy comes from general funds, the Colonial Secretary must grant the extension of time, after hearing the Council of State.

At the end of the extension, the concession shall be forfeited, if within that period the stipulations are not carried out.

(Articles 49 and 85 of the Regulations.)

ART. 86. When by the fault of the company the public service of a subsidized work is interrupted, the Colonial Secretary, the Deputations, or the Municipal Council, as the case may be, shall immediately adopt the necessary measures to assure its provisional operation at the expense of the concessionaire.

Within six months the company must prove that it has sufficient resources to continue the operation, which it may assign to another company or to a third person, after previous special authorization of the Government or the proper corporation. If even by these means the service is not continued, the concession shall be considered forfeited. (Articles 50 and 85 of the Regulations.)

ART. 87. From the resolution of the Government declaring forfeiture the concessionaire may appeal, by the administrative jurisdiction on contests, within the period of two months from the day on which he may have been notified. When this period has passed without an appeal being made, the decision of the Government shall be considered as consented to.

The concessionaires may also appeal by the administrative jurisdiction of contests, within the same time, from the decision of forfeiture which, according to its powers, may be made by the Deputations or the Municipal Councils, after the appeal to the Government shall have been exhausted, in the manner prescribed by the Law. (Articles 48 and 85 of the Regulations.)

ART. 88. When a forfeiture of a subsidized concession is finally declared, the executed works shall be offered to public bids for the term of three months. The basis for these bids shall be the value, according to appraisal, of the lands acquired, of the completed works, and of the materials of construction and operation thereof, deducting the amounts which, as aid or subsidy, may have been given to the concessionaire in lands, works, cash, or other kind of property. (Articles 51 and 85 of the Regulations.)

ART. 89. If, at the auction referred to by the preceding article, there should be no bidder, a new auction shall be advertised for the period of two months, on the basis of two-thirds of the amount of the appraisal. If even then the sale should be prevented because there were no bidders, it shall be announced the third and last time, for a period of one month, at a fixed amount. (Articles 51 and 85 of the Regulations.)

ART. 90. If at any of the three auctions referred to in the previous articles, propositions admissible within the advertised terms shall be made, the work shall be awarded to the best bidder, who shall give in guarantee 5 per cent of the amount of the works which are incompleted, and shall receive the concession under the same conditions as were granted in the forfeited one, being substituted to the previous concessionaire in all his rights and obligations, and subject to the provisions of the present Law. (Articles 51 and 85 of the Regulations.)

ART. 91. From the proceeds of the works publicly sold, which shall be paid by the concessionaire, in the manner prescribed by the previous article, there shall be deducted the expenses of the appraisal and sale, and the rest shall be turned over to whomsoever it may belong. (Articles 51 and 85 of the Regulations.)

ART. 92. In case the concession should not be awarded at any of the three auctions, the State, Province, or town in whose charge the work may be, shall take charge of all which may have been constructed, and shall continue, if it deems it proper, by means of a new concession, which shall be granted in all things in conformity to the provisions of this Law, without the first concessionaire in such case having any right to any indemnity whatsoever.

(Articles 51 and 85 of the Regulations.)

CHAPTER VIII.

CONCESSIONS OF THE PUBLIC DOMAIN AND OF THE DOMAIN OF THE STATE.

ART. 93. Concessions which individuals or companies request for the execution of works which have constantly to occupy or use a part of the public domain devoted to general use, shall in all cases be made by the Colonial Department, which shall follow the provisions established for this purpose in Chapter VI and in Chapter VII of this Law, according to whether there are involved subsidized works or those for the execution of which an aid of some sort is asked from the public funds.

(Article 122 of the Regulations.)

ART. 94. Individuals or companies who ask for a concession of the public domain for the construction of a work of general or private use shall direct their petition to the Colonial Department or its delegates, with a project made in accordance with the Regulations for the execution of this Law.

The Colonial Department shall examine the investigations which go to prove the established rights in the public domain which it is desired to occupy, the advantages or inconveniences which might result to the general interests from this work, and the other circumstances which it may be desirable to take into account before the granting of the concession; all of which shall be done in accordance with the provisions of the special laws and of the Regulations.

(Articles 123, 124, 125, 134, and 135 of the Regulations.)

ART. 95. If, from the investigation referred to in the preceding article, it should appear that the work in question does not hinder or impede the use of the public domain affected thereby, the concession may be granted by the Colonial Department or its delegates, in accordance with the provisions of the special laws of the several works, adding among the general provisions the following:

First. The time in which the works shall commence and be completed.

Second. The conditions for the establishment and use of the work and the consequences of failure to comply with these conditions.

Third. The guarantee which the concessionaire shall give in order to secure the fulfillment of the stipulated provisions.

Fourth. The cases in which the concession may be declared forfeited, as well as the consequences of such forfeiture.

Fifth. The establishment of maximum rates designated for the use and profit of the works.

(Article 126 of the Regulations.)

ART. 96. If, before any decision shall be made concerning the petitions of the public domain referred to in the preceding articles, there should be another or other petitions incompatible with the first, the Colonial Department shall select those which offer the best terms to the public interests, for which purpose an investigation of the competing projects shall be held, in the manner determined by the Regulations.

In similar cases, nevertheless, and in those in which it is not believed to be opportune because of special circumstances, the Colonial Department may decide that the concession be given, after a public bidding, in accordance with the provisions of Articles 97 and 98. ·

(Articles 127, 128, 129, 130, 131, 132, and 133 of the Regulations.)

ART. 97. If, from the investigation referred to in Article 94, it should appear that the work does not hinder or impede the use and profit to which the part of the public domain affected by the work may be devoted, the concession may also be granted by the Colonial Department when it is thus deemed proper for the general interests.

The concession, in the case of the present article, shall always be made after public bidding, which shall be based in the first place on the reductions in the rates approved for the use and profit of the work; and in case of equality of these rates, on the raising of the price which shall previously have been designated for the part of the public domain which shall have to be ceded.

(Articles 135 and 136 of the Regulations.)

ART. 98. The conditions of the concession when, in accordance with the previous article, it shall have been made through public bidding, shall be those indicated in Article 95; adding that the person to whom the award is made shall be obliged, when he is not the same one who presented the project, to pay the petitioner the expenses which said project may have occasioned him, according to expert appraisal made and published previously to the public sale.

(Article 137 of the Regulations.)

ART. 99. When, for the concessions of the class referred to in Article 97, two or more petitions may have been presented, the Colonial Secretary shall select, by the procedure determined by Article 96, the one which appears most proper to serve as the basis of the public biddings which must determine to whom the concessions shall finally be granted.

(Article 138 of the Regulations.)

ART. 100. The concessions referred to in the previous articles of this Chapter shall be granted for ninety-nine years at most, except in the cases wherein the special laws of public works establish a longer period, or when the concession is granted by means of a special law which may thus determine.

In all cases these concessions shall be understood to be made without prejudice to third parties and protecting vested rights. The concessionaire shall consequently be responsible for the damages and injuries which the work may occasion to private property or to the part of the public domain not occupied by him.

(Article 139 of the Regulations.)

ART. 101. When the concession is granted and the guaranty is deposited, an instrument shall be executed in which shall appear the grant of the concession and the stipulated conditions; certifying besides to the deposit of the guaranty, and adding a printed and authorized copy of this Law and of the Regulations for its execution.

(Article 139 of the Regulations.)

ART. 102. The concessionaire may transfer his concession or freely alienate the works, it being understood, however, that the one who substitutes him in his rights also substitutes him in his obligations imposed by the provisions of the concession, and that the guaranties which he may have made to cover his liability remain in existence.

Of the alienation or transfer of the rights belonging to the concessionaire, an account shall be given to the Colonial Department, or to the corporation which might have granted the concession, for the proper purposes.

(Article 139 of the Regulations.)

ART. 103. When the concession is made, the Administration shall have the right to see that the stipulated conditions are absolutely fulfilled, as well during the execution of the works as during their operation.

The guaranty referred to in the third paragraph of Article 95 shall be returned to the concessionnaire when he proves that he has completed the works, and this shall be made to appear in his document of concession.

(Article 139 of the Regulations.)

ART. 104. The declaration of forfeiture of the concession of the public domain, in a proper case, shall be pronounced by the Colonial Secretary, after proceedings have been had, in which the interested party shall be especially heard. The consequences of the forfeiture shall be those which for similar cases are established in Chapters VI and VII of this Law.

When the forfeiture is declared, the instrument granting the concession shall be null, and shall be surrendered.

(Article 139 of the Regulations.)

ART. 105. When a work which shall permanently occupy a part of the public domain, in which there is no public use or profit whatever, is to be carried out by individuals or companies, the administrative authorization which the Colonial Secretary or his delegates is authorized to grant shall be sufficient, in accordance with the provisions of special laws and of the Regulations.

(Articles 141, 142, 143, and 144 of the Regulations.)

ART. 106. The person requesting the authorization referred to in the preceding article shall accompany with his petition a plan in which shall appear the object of the work, the part of the public domain it is intended to occupy, and an estimate of the works.

This project shall pass through the proceedings prescribed by special laws and the Regulations before the authorization shall be granted.

(Article 140 of the Regulations.)

ART. 107. When, for the execution or operation of a work requested by individuals or companies, it shall be necessary to occupy permanently a part of the public domain devoted to general use, there shall first be also obtained the authorization of the Colonial Secretary or his delegates. This authorization may be granted without demanding any guaranty or the presentation of the project, and by the brief proceedings which are designated by the Regulations.

(Article 145 of the Regulations.)

ART. 108. The administrative authorization is also needed for the execution or operation of a work which affects established servitudes on private property for the benefit of the public domain.

This authorization shall be granted by the Colonial Secretary or his delegates, as in the case of the preceding article; but it may be perpetual, saving always the rights of private property.

(Article 145 of the Regulations.)

ART. 109. For the works devoted to the operation of a private industry, the occupation of matters connected with the public domain may be granted, in accordance with the provisions of this general Law and the special laws of public works; when the concession referred to in the preceding paragraph has been made, the individual or company obtaining it may construct the work and make use of it in the manner in which it may be deemed convenient, without further intervention on the part of the Government than that relating to the safety, policing, and management of the public domain.

(Article 146 of the Regulations.)

ART. 110. When, for the execution of a work, by companies or individuals, devoted to public or to private use, there may be occupied a part of the public domain of the State, the previous concession of the Colonial Secretary shall be necessary, in accordance with the provisions of the articles of this Chapter treating of public domain; but always with the indispensable prerequisite that there be public bidding, at which the project of the petitioner shall serve as the basis.

The bidding shall have for its object the determination of the amount which the concessionaire shall have to pay for the domain ceded, and shall take place in accordance with the formalities necessary for the sale of public lands, the concession being granted to the best bidder.

The petitioner shall have the right of preference on equal terms at the bidding, and, in case he shall not take the concession, of being indemnified by the person to whom it is awarded, for the expenses of the project, according to expert appraisal made and published before the public sale.

(Article 147 of the Regulations.)

ART. 111. The authorization of the Colonial Secretary is necessary to execute or operate a work which changes servitudes established in the domain of the State.

This authorization shall be ceded in conformity with similar proceedings to those established by Article 108 of this Law.

(Article 148 of the Regulations.)

ART. 112. The resolutions concerning concessions by competent authority of the public domain and of the domain of the State, shall be final, saving the appeals which may be proper according to the Laws.

CHAPTER IX.

DECLARATION OF PUBLIC UTILITY.

ART. 113. Before the execution of any work devoted to public use, whoever may construct it, there shall be the declaration of public utility.

From this formality are excepted:

First. The works which are in charge of the State and which are carried out in accordance with the provisions of Chapter III of the present Law.

Second. The works included in the general provincial or municipal plans, designated in Articles 19, 33, and 43 of the Law.

Third. Every work, of whatsoever kind, the construction of which may have been authorized by special law.

No work devoted to private use can be declared of public utility.

(Article 149 of the Regulations.)

ART. 114. The declaration of public utility shall carry with it, so far as the individuals who request it are concerned:

First. The right of neighborhood for the builders and their employees, which consists of the use of the objects enjoyed in common in the district of the towns in which the works are situated.

Second. The application of the law of eminent domain to private property in accordance with the provisions of the said Law and of the Regulations for its execution.

Third. The exemption from the land tax and the property tax on the transfers of property which may take place in consequence of the application of the said law of eminent domain.

The declaration of public utility may also carry with it the exemption from other temporary or permanent taxes, whenever it is thus determined by a special law for each case.

(Article 150 of the Regulations.)

ART. 115. The declaration of public utility, when it shall have been made in accordance with the provisions of Article 113 and shall carry with it the application of the law of eminent domain, shall be made by the legislative power in relation to works which, in the judgment of the Government, are of great importance; by the Colonial Department in reference to works paid for by the general funds of the State, the budgets of which are approved, and by the Governor-General in reference to provincial and municipal works, which may embrace the territory of two or more provinces, and which may be submitted to his resolution according to Article 45; by the Governor-General in reference to State, provincial, or municipal works, the projects of which may be approved by his authority, according to this law, and by the respective Governors in what refers to provincial and municipal works which are within the territory of his jurisdiction.

In case the exercise of the right of eminent domain is not requested, the Municipal Councils shall have the right to make the declaration of public utility when the work is municipal, and is included in one municipal district; the Provincial Deputations shall make the declaration when the work is provincial, and when, being municipal, it is included in two or more towns; and lastly, the Colonial Secretary or the Governor-General, respectively, when the work is in charge of the State, and when, being provincial, it shall embrace territories belonging to more than one province.

(Articles 152, 153, 154, 155, 156, 157, 158, and 159 of the Regulations.)

ART. 116. The individual or company which asks for the declaration of public utility of a work shall annex to his or its petition a complete project, so that judgment thereof may be formed, and of its object, of the private property which it shall occupy, and of the advantages which shall accrue to the general interests.

(Article 151 of the Regulations.)

ART. 117. Before adopting a resolution, the project shall be submitted to an investigation, in which shall be heard, in the first place, all those interested in the condemnation proceedings, if the application of the law of eminent domain is requested, and afterwards the other individuals, officers, and corporations that, for each case, are specified in the Regulations.

When the investigation has been made, in the cases in which the declaration of public utility is to be declared by the Cortes, the Colonial Secretary shall present the proper form of law. As to the rest, the Colonial Secretary, his delegates, or the proper corporation shall decide upon the declaration requested, as may be deemed proper.

(Articles 152, 153, 154, 155, 156, 157, 158, and 159 of the Regulations.)

ART. 118. The resolutions which, in relation to public utility, may be adopted by the competent central Provincial or Municipal Administration shall be final, saving the appeals which are proper in accordance with the Law.

(Article 160 of the Regulations.)

CHAPTER X.

COMPETENCY OF JURISDICTION IN MATTERS CONNECTED WITH PUBLIC WORKS.

ART. 119. The administrative jurisdiction to hear disputes shall hear the appeals against the rulings of the Administration—

First. When the forfeiture of a concession made to individuals or companies in the terms prescribed by this law is declared.

Second. In all those cases in which the administrative resolutions which are final affect rights acquired by virtue of rulings emanating from the same Administration.

ART. 120. The tribunals of justice shall have jurisdiction of—

First. Questions which may arise between the Administration and individuals concerning the public domain or private property, and concerning servitudes founded on titles of civil rights.

Second. Questions which may arise between individuals concerning the preferred right to the public domain, according to the present law, when the preference is founded on titles of civil rights.

Third. Questions relative to damages and injuries occasioned to a third person in his property right, the alienation of which is not compellable under the right of eminent domain, by reason of the establishment or use of the works which are the subject of the concession, or for any other causes depending on the concession.

CHAPTER XI.

GENERAL PROVISIONS.

ART. 121. Foreign capital which is employed in public works and in the acquisition of lands necessary for them, shall be exempt from reprisals, confiscations, and embargoes by reason of war.

ART. 122. The provisions of the present Law do not invalidate any of the rights acquired prior to its publication and in accordance with the legislation on which they may have been founded.

ART. 123. The proceedings relative to public works which, on the publication of these Laws, may be pending, shall be carried out in accordance with the prior legislation under which they were started, unless the interested parties prefer to submit to the provisions of the present Law.

In case there are several interested parties, and they do not agree, the proceedings shall follow the provisions of the former legislation.

ART. 124. The Colonial Secretary, after hearing the Secretary of the Navy regarding matters of ports which affect the services depending on that Department, and by himself in the others, but always after a report of the Consulting Board of Roads, Canals, and Ports, and after hearing the full Council of State, may decide that the special laws published in the Peninsula relative to railroads, highroads, waters, and ports may be extended to the Colonies, and of the Regulations and instructions for their application, introducing in them the modifications which he may deem proper; but always after the report of the Consulting Board of Roads, Canals, and Ports, and after hearing the full Council of State.

ART. 125. All laws, decrees, and other prior provisions affecting public works which may be in conflict with the present Law are hereby repealed.

Madrid, April 19, 1883.

The Colonial Department, under date of the 26th of last April, communicates to His Excellency, the Governor-General, the following Royal Order:

YOUR EXCELLENCY: In compliance with Article 2 of the Royal Decree of the 19th instant, ordering that the General Law of Public Works be applied to the Island of Cuba, His Majesty, the King (whom God preserve), in conformity with what has been consulted with the full Council of State, has seen fit to approve the annexed Regulations for the execution and fulfillment of said law. By Royal Order I communicate it to Your Excellency for your information and consequent action.

And the approval of His Excellency having been given on the 19th of the present month, by his superior order there follows the publication of the said Regulations, for general information.

Habana, May 30, 1883.

The Secretary of the General Government.

M. DIAZ DE LA QUINTANA.

31

REGULATIONS FOR THE EXECUTION OF THE GENERAL LAW OF PUBLIC WORKS OF THE ISLAND OF CUBA.

TITLE FIRST.

WORKS IN CHARGE OF THE STATE.

CHAPTER I.

PROJECTS AND CONSTRUCTION OF WORKS BY THE METHOD OF ORDINARY CONTRACTS.

ART. 1. In accordance with Article 4 of the General Law and the special laws for each kind of works, the following are in charge of the State:

First. Highroads, railroads, and ports included in the corresponding plans.

Second. Light-houses for the illumination of the coast, and the establishment of all kinds of maritime signals.

Third. The work of retaining within their beds and making navigable the principal rivers, and the drainage of lakes and marshes belonging to the State.

Fourth. Civil constructions for the service of the Administration of the State.

(Article 4 of the Law.)

ART. 2. The Colonial Secretary, who has the administrative management of the works designated in the preceding article, shall make the plans of those which are in charge of the State, following the proceedings laid down in the proper Regulations for the execution of the laws of highroads, railroads, and ports.

(Article 19 of the Law.)

ART. 3. The Colonial Secretary, in conformity with the provisions of Article 22 of the General Law, shall order the study of the works included in the plans of the State, in the order in which they are respectively mentioned and according to the legislative credits which admit of it.

(Article 22 of the Law.)

ART. 4. When the study of any work shall be necessary, the Governor-General may give the proper order to the Inspector-General of Public Works, who shall communicate it to the Engineer of the respective Province. Said Engineer shall make the estimate of the expenses which the study may necessitate, and shall submit it for superior approval. The Governor-General shall give this approval when the amount does not exceed 5,000 pesos, and the Colonial Secretary shall do so in all other cases.

(Article 20 of the Law.)

ART. 5. Whenever the work affects the territories of two or more provinces, the Chief Engineers of each two contiguous provinces must beforehand as to the connecting points which it is advisable to adopt. If there be disagreement, the Colonial Secretary shall decide on reports of the said Chiefs and after hearing the Consulting Board of Roads, Canals, and Ports. After the said point has been decided, each engineer shall proceed independently within his territory. In the said case, the Colonial Secretary, when he shall deem it opportune, may order the direction of the plan to be intrusted to one of the two Chief Engineers, or he may appoint for the purpose another member of the Corps.

(Article 22 of the Law.)

ART. 6. Every project must consist of the following documents:

First. Explanatory memorial.

Second. Plans.

Third. Articles of technical conditions.

Fourth. Estimate.

This last document shall include, besides the cost of the work, the amounts which it may be considered necessary for condemnation proceedings, and the drainage necessary for the foundations of hydraulic works, as well as all the other dependencies of the work, with the object of forming an idea of the total cost.

When the projected work may be operated, with earnings, there shall be accompanied the schedule of rates which are to be established for its use and profit, and the basis on which the application of the proposed schedule is to be made, as well as a calculation of the proposed gain to the company.

The projects of the works shall be made in accordance with the forms which govern at the time of their formation, as well as the general rules of the service and the special instructions which in each case the general Direction may deem it convenient to establish.

(Articles 22 and 26 of the Law.)

ART. 7. For works of ports, besides the formalities expressed in the preceding article, those provided by the special law concerning the preliminary plans and investigations, which must precede the drafting of the final projects, must be observed.

(Article 22 of the Law.)

ART. 8. Works of repair can not be carried out until after the approval of the estimates made by the Chief Engineers of the Province, in accordance with the instructions which exist for this kind of service.

For the preservation of the existing works in charge of the State the Chief Engineers shall draft annual estimates, which, with ample time, shall be sent through the General Inspection for the proper approval.

(Article 32 of the Law.)

ART. 9. When a work not included in the plans of the State is under consideration, the execution of which shall nevertheless be deemed proper in the judgment of the Government, the Colonial Secretary shall order that the Engineers make a preliminary project of the work.

This preliminary project shall be drawn in accordance with the instructions which may be given in each case, and shall always consist of a memorial and plans which give a clear idea of the work and of its principal details, with an idea of its cost.

If the work affects more than two provinces, the rules fixed in article 5 as to connecting points shall be taken into consideration in the drafting of the preliminary project, of which as many copies shall be made as there may be provinces interested in the work.

(Articles 20 and 22 of the Law.)

ART. 10. The preliminary project referred to in the preceding article shall be submitted to an investigation concerning the propriety or necessity of the execution of the work, in which shall be heard—

First. All those individuals who may be interested in the work, for which purpose it shall be exhibited in the office of the Secretary of the General Government for a period which shall be announced in the Boletines Oficiales of the respective provinces, and which shall be not less than thirty days.

Second. The Municipal Councils and the Deputations of the localities and provinces affected by the work.

Third. The Boards of Agriculture, Industry, and Commerce of the said Provinces.

Fourth. The military authorities, the naval authorities, and the Provincial Health Boards in special cases in which it is necessary, because demanded by the nature of the work.

Fifth. The Engineers in charge of the service and the Chief Engineers of the Provinces, so that they may make explanations concerning the claims which may have been made during the investigation.

Said investigation shall be sent in each province by the Governor of the same to the Governor-General of the Island, with his own opinion, and he, after hearing the General Inspection of Public Works and the Consulting Board of the Island, shall send it with his report to the Colonial Secretary.

All the above-named documents shall be sent to the Consulting Board of Roads, Canals, and Ports for the proper report thereon.

(Articles 20 and 22 of the Law.)

ART. 11. If, in view of the result of the investigation referred to in the preceding article, it may be deemed convenient or necessary to execute the work in question, the Colonial Secretary shall present to the Cortes the form of law which in this case is necessary, in order to undertake the work, in accordance with the provisions of Article 20 of the general Law of Public Works. When this authorization has been once granted, the final study shall be made, which shall follow the proceedings set forth in Articles 3 to 7 of the present Regulations.

(Articles 20 and 22 of the Law.)

ART. 12. If the work should be of admitted urgency, after the requisites provided by Article 20 of the Law shall have been fulfilled, the Colonial Secretary shall decide upon the immediate drafting of the project, without waiting for the making of the estimate of the studies referred to in Article 4 of these Regulations, without prejudice that, as soon as possible, the said estimate shall be made and sent for superior approval.

(Articles 20 and 22 of the Law.)

ART. 13. In fulfillment of the provisions of the general Law of Public Works, the Government shall not include in the general budgets—

First. The credits necessary for the preservation of all existing works in charge of the State, in view of the estimates which the General Inspectors of Public Works, through the General Government, must annually send for this purpose, as provided by Article 8 of these Regulations.

Second. The credits demanded by the repair of said works, according to the estimates mentioned in the same article.

Third. The amounts necessary for new works, the execution of which is properly authorized in accordance with Articles 20 and 21 of the general Law, and the projects of which are properly approved; said amounts shall include the probable expenses of condemnation proceedings, drainage, and other matters referred to in Article 6 of the present Regulations.

Fourth. The sums which may be reasonably judged necessary to carry out the projects of new works, and of repairs which might have been studied during the corresponding economic year.

Fifth. The amount for the works which it might be necessary to execute because of admitted urgency, in accordance with the provisions of said Article 20 of the general Law.

(Article 21 of the Law.)

ART. 14. The Colonial Secretary shall decide on the method which must be followed in constructing a public work in charge of the State, subject to the provisions of Article 24 of the general Law, and also, in a proper case, to the provisions of the Royal Decree of the 5th of May, 1876, after the Engineers, who may have drawn the project, shall have been heard, as well as the Chief Engineer of the Province or of the proper service, and of the Consulting Board.

(Article 24 of the Law.)

ART. 15. If the work should have to be executed by the method of management, it shall be constructed by the Engineers of Roads, Canals, and Ports, in accordance with the provisions which exist or might exist in this branch of the service.

If the work shall have to be carried out by the method of contract, the Engineers of the State shall have the right to superintend the construction, in order to see that the special conditions are carried out, make the provisional and the final acceptance, as well as the final estimate; all of which is prescribed by the Regulations of the service.

(Article 29 of the Law.)

ART. 16. If the work shall have to be executed by contract, the public bidding which shall precede it shall be made in accordance with the provisions existing for the contracting for such public service and the Regulations established for that purpose, for those which specially belong to the Colonial Department.

ART. 17. In the construction of every public work which shall be carried out by the contract method, and in accordance with the first of the methods indicated in Article 25 of the general Law, there shall govern—

First. The general conditions established, or which in the future may be established, for all kinds of contracts for public works in charge of the Colonial Department.

Second. The technical conditions which form part of the project and which have been approved, together with the latter.

Third. The particular and economic conditions which in each case the Colonial Department or the Governor-General may establish, in which shall be stated in detail, besides the special clauses which the nature of each contract might demand, the guarantee which is to be given by the contractor as security for the carrying out of his obligations, the times, manner, and places in which payments are to be made, the dates on which the work shall be begun and finished, and the time for which the contractor has to guarantee and be responsible for the solidity and stability of the executed works.

(Article 25 of the Law.)

ART. 18. The studies of projects and the execution of works which are included under the classification of civil constructions devoted to service depending on the Colonial Department shall be carried out in accordance with the provisions of this chapter concerning public works in general, without other distinction than that the architects who shall have charge of said construction, shall do the work which in the other case is in charge of the Engineers of Roads, Canals, and Ports.

(Article 28 of the Law.)

CHAPTER II.

CONCESSIONS FOR THE CONSTRUCTION WITHOUT SUBSIDY OF WORKS INCLUDED IN THE GENERAL PLANS OF THE STATE.

ART 19. Concessions of public works in charge of the State which are included in the plans of the same, and which are asked for without aid or subsidy of any kind, shall be made by the Colonial Department

to the companies or individuals who may request them, after the proceedings laid down by these Regulations.
(Article 53 of the Law.)

ART. 20. The granting of every concession mentioned in the preceding article shall only be after the drafting of the proper project. If there is no project drawn by the Engineers of the Government for the work in question, it may be left to private initiative to make the studies, as provided by Article 56 of the general Law of Public Works.
(Article 56 of the Law.)

ART. 21. In the case of the preceding article, the individual or company that may desire to draw the project, shall petition the Colonial Department asking for the proper authorization, which may be given him after he has made a guaranty to pay for the damages which his operations may cause, the amount of which may be fixed, keeping in mind the importance of the project and the special circumstances of the ground which it is to occupy.

In case the authorization is granted, a period shall be fixed for the presentation of the project, the order being published in the Gaceta de la Habana and the Boletines Oficiales of the interested provinces.

The petitioner to whom this authorization is granted shall enjoy all the advantages which in such cases are granted by Article 56 of the Law, and shall present the project to the Colonial Department or the General Government within the limited time. If this is not done, the authorization which has been granted shall be considered annulled, unless the petitioner shall have asked for and obtained an extension of time for this purpose, which shall only be granted once, all petitions for further extension being ignored.

The guaranty shall be returned to the petitioner when he presents the project, after a certificate showing that he has satisfied all damages which he may have occasioned.

Every individual or company may for itself study the projects of works included in the plans of the State without the authority referred to in Article 56 of the general Law, but in such case it shall have no right to the advantages granted by said article.
(Articles 55 and 56 of the Law.)

ART. 22. The projects drawn by individuals for works referred to in the preceding articles shall consist of the same documents and be drawn in accordance with the same forms and provisions which are demanded for the works of the State, as provided by Article 6 of these Regulations.
(Article 55 of the Law.)

ART. 23. On presenting a project to the Colonial Department or to the General Government, the individual or company that shall have drawn it shall also present, as a guaranty of the fulfillment of his or its obligations, the document which shows that he or it has deposited in the proper place an amount equivalent to 1 per cent of the total estimate for the execution of the work. The General Office of Adminis-tration and Public Works of the said Department or the Secretary of the General Government of the island, shall give a receipt for the project to the interested party, stating the day and the hour on which it may have been presented. This receipt shall constitute prima facie proof for every question of priority which may arise in the course of the proceedings.

(Article 57 of the Law.)

ART. 24. The project shall then be sent to the Chief Engineer of the Province, in order that he may go over it on the ground for the purpose of determining exactly the facts which it contains. The expenses which this may entail shall be paid by the petitioner, who shall deposit their amount in the Treasury of the Province or in the General Treasury of the island before this work is begun.

Of the result of the comparison, as well as of the other details of the project, the Engineer shall give a detailed report, which shall be sent to the respective Governor, to be attached to the other papers.

Thereafter an investigation shall be made directly by the Governors of the interested Provinces, concerning the propriety of making the concession, and concerning the proposed rates for the use and profit of the works. In this investigation individuals who might consider them-selves interested shall be heard orally, and they may be compelled to answer interrogatories which may be specially framed for each partic-ular case. Thereafter the corporations and officials who, according to the importance and nature of the works, it may be deemed convenient to consult, shall be heard in writing; and in all cases there shall be heard the Provincial Deputations and the Chief Engineers of the corre-sponding Provinces or services.

The Governors shall send the reports, with their own opinions, to the Governor-General, who, with his opinion, and after complying with the proper legal steps, shall send it to the Colonial Secretary, enclosing the projects which he may have received from the Chief Engineers.

(Article 58 of the Law.)

ART. 25. When the project refers to ports, besides the formalities established in the preceding article, those shall be observed which are established for this purpose by the special Law of Ports and the Regu-lations for its execution.

(Article 58 of the Law.)

ART. 26. On fulfilling the provisions of the preceding articles, the Consulting Board of Roads, Canals, and Ports shall be heard, which shall give an opinion concerning the project and the rates, and the basis on which they may have made an investigation.

When these formalities have been complied with, the concession may be granted, if proper, in view of the result of the proceedings, by means of a Royal Decree through the Colonial Secretary drawing the proper instrument, which shall be delivered to the concessionaire.

(Article 58 of the Law.)

ART. 27. No variation or modification whatever shall be introduced in the approved project for a concession of this class, without the proper authorization of the Colonial Secretary, after hearing the opinion of the Consulting Board of Roads, Canals, and Ports.

(Article 58 of the Law.)

ART. 28. In every concession, besides the technical conditions of the project for the execution of the work and those of the general ones which may be applicable, there shall govern other particular conditions, in which shall be included the special ones which govern contracts of public works which may be considered proper, according to the result of the proceedings; and there must appear among them the following:

First. The designation of the guaranty which the concessionaire shall give in security for the fulfillment of his obligations. This guaranty shall be from 3 to 5 per cent of the amount of the estimate, and shall not be returned to the interested party until he has proved the construction of the works and the supply of materials to the value of one-third at least of the total cost of the work, according to appraisement made by the Engineers in charge of the superintendence of the work, applying to those which may have been made the prices of the approved estimate.

The guaranty in every case shall be made where contracted, within the term of one month from the date of the granting of the concession, on the penalty of the loss by the concessionaire of all right, including that of the deposit, if this shall not have been done.

Second. The dates on which the concessionaire shall commence and complete the works, as well as the progress with which they shall be constructed in given periods, in order that they may be concluded within the time provided for.

Third. The schedule of rates which may have been approved for the use and profit of the works, as well as the basis for their application.

Fourth. The time during which the concessionaire shall have the right to enjoy the proceeds of the rates referrred to in the preceding article, which can not exceed ninety-nine years.

Fifth. The cases of forfeiture of the concession.

Besides this, it must be seen that the concession shall be granted without prejudice to the third party and saving private rights.

(Articles 59 and 66 of the Law.)

ART. 29. Every concession of this kind shall be forfeited if any of the special conditions designated in the preceding article are not complied with, if the preservation of the works during their operation is not properly attended to, and if the operation is not carried on in accordance with the terms agreed upon.

The case provided in Article 60 of the general Law of Public Works shall also be a case of forfeiture.

The declaration of forfeiture shall be made by the Colonial Department, after proceedings in which there shall be heard the concessionaire, the Consulting Board of Roads, Canals, and Ports, and the Colonial Department of the Council of State. From this decision the interested party may appeal by means of the administrative jurisdiction of contests.

(Articles 59 and 67 of the Law.)

ART. 30. When the forfeiture of a concession has been declared, the Engineers who may have been designated by the Governor-General, shall proceed to make an estimate of the works completed and the materials furnished and their valuation, according to the prices of the approved estimates.

The measurement and the valuation, accompanied by an explanatory memorial and plans which show the state in which the works are found at the time, shall be sent to the Colonial Department for its approval, after report of the Consulting Board of Roads, Canals, and Ports.

(Article 67 of the Law.)

ART. 31. To every concession which is declared forfeited, there shall be immediately applied articles 68 to 71, both inclusive, of the General Law of Public Works; and for the purpose of the public bidding on the executed works, the valuation made and approved in accordance with the provisions of the preceding article shall serve as a basis.

(Articles 68, 69, 70, and 71 of the Law.)

ART. 32. During the period set forth in Article 63 of the Law of Public Works, there shall be admitted in the General Government of the Island all the projects presented by individuals or companies to carry on the work, the concession of which may have been requested.

In said case, in order that the projects may be admitted, they shall be accompanied by a document which proves that the deposit of 1 per cent designated in Article 23 of these Regulations has been made. The admitted projects shall be submitted to all the provisions of Articles 22, 24, and 25 of these Regulations.

(Article 63 of the Law.)

ART. 33. When more than one project shall have been presented for the same work, there shall be a comparison on the ground made for each one of them; and the investigations provided by Article 24 shall include the advantages or disadvantages which may result from their comparison, in order to ascertain which is preferable. The same object shall be kept in mind by the Consulting Board of Roads, Canals, and Ports, or by the Royal Academy of San Fernando, as the case may be, on investigating the proceedings of the concession in the manner provided by Article 26.

When the report shall have been made by the proper Corporation, the proceedings shall pass to the Colonial Department of the Council of State, and after this requisite has been complied with there shall be decided by Royal Decree the preference which shall in each case be given to one of the several competing projects, in order to grant its author the concession requested.

The petitioner or petitioners whose projects shall have been rejected shall have no right to any claim or indemnity whatsoever.

(Article 61 of the Law.)

ART. 34. When, from the investigations instituted, there should result an equality among the conditions of two or more projects presented for the same work, the concession shall be made after public bidding and on the basis of the project which shall first have been presented to the Colonial Department or to the General Government of the Island, excepting the modifications introduced therein in consequence of examinations which shall have been made in compliance with the provisions of these Regulations.

The petitioner of the first project shall in such case show his acceptance of the modifications introduced and his consent to the bidding. If he shall refuse to do either, his project shall be ignored and it shall be returned to him, together with the deposit which he may have made.

Then the person who presented the second project shall have this privilege, and so on, observing the same procedure; and if none of the petitioners signifies his acceptance, it shall be declared that there will be no grant of the concession.

(Article 61 of the Law.)

ART. 35. When the Colonial Department shall have once decided that the concession be granted after public bids, before announcing the sale, the project which shall serve as the basis of the bidding, in accordance with the provisions of the preceding article, shall be appraised.

The appraisement shall be made independently by experts named, one by the Governor-General of the Island and the other by the interested petitioner. In case of disagreement, a third shall be named by agreement of these two; and if this agreement can not be reached, the appointment shall be made by the proper judicial authority.

In the appraisal there shall be included the material expenses of all kinds occasioned by the drawing of the project, and also the proper interest on the principal advanced to pay for these expenses. To the appraisal thus made, shall be added the fees of the experts. When the appraisal has thus been made, it shall be sent for the approval of the Colonial Secretary, who, before rendering a decision, shall hear the Consulting Board of Roads, Canals, and Ports.

(Article 62 of the Law.)

ART. 36. When the amount of the value of the project has been determined, the public sale of the concession shall be announced for a period determined by the Colonial Secretary; and at this sale there may take part not only the authors of the projects presented, but also all those who may desire the concession, providing they show that they have made the deposit of one per cent of the estimate of the works.

The bidding shall take place in Havana in the office of the General Government, and shall be based in the first place on reductions in the schedules of rates of the concession which may have been fixed, in the manner prescribed by the third paragraph of Article 28.

The proposals shall be sealed, and in strict accordance with the form which shall be presented, wherein shall appear in writing the per cent of reduction which the bidder agrees to make on the amount fixed for the sale, this percentage being the same and the only percentage for all parts of the schedule.

When the propositions presented shall have been read, the person who signed the one offering the greatest reduction shall be declared the best bidder, and a minute of the sale shall be made, which shall be sent for the approval of the Colonial Secretary.

(Article 62 of the Law.)

ART. 37. If from the reading of the propositions it should appear that two or more equally advantageous ones have been presented, there shall immediately be a new open bidding, in which only those shall take part who have signed equal propositions. This bidding shall be based on the reduction of the number of years which, in accordance with paragraph 4 of Article 28 of these Regulations, shall have been fixed for the concession, and shall last at least fifteen minutes, after which it shall terminate when the President so orders, after having given warning three times.

(Article 62 of the Law.)

ART. 38. In all matters not expressly modified by the preceding articles, the instructions approved the 11th of September, 1869, for the conduct of public biddings for public service and works of the Colonial Department in the Island, shall govern, it being understood that the deposit to take part in the bidding shall only be required from those who are not authors of projects previously presented and not withdrawn or returned for lack of fulfillment of the requisites referred to in Article 34 of these Regulations.

The petitioner whose project shall serve as the basis of the bids, shall reserve the right in all cases of preference on equal terms, and, in consequence thereof, of being declared the person to whom the concession is awarded for the amount which shall have been offered by the best bidder. In order to exercise this privilege he shall take part, either personally or by representative duly authorized, in the bidding, which shall be extended for half an hour, in order that the interested party may make the proper declaration, which, in a proper case, shall be stated in the minutes of the bidding. If this half hour shall elapse without a declaration being made, it shall be understood that the petitioner renounces the right to preference on equal terms, and the President shall declare the best bidder the signer of the proposition which is most advantageous.

(Articles 62 and 72 of the Law.)

ART. 39. If the person to whom the award is made shall not be the signer of the proposition whose project shall serve as the basis of the bids, he shall be obliged to pay the latter, within the period of one month, the amount of the appraisal of the project made in the manner prescribed by Article 35 of these Regulations.

(Article 62 of the Law.)

ART. 40. When one of the concessions included in the present chapter of these Regulations shall be granted, Engineers of the Government shall have the supervision of the execution of the works, in order that they may be constructed in accordance with the approved plans. In the same manner they shall have the supervision of the inspection before the work is turned over to the public service, making a minute of this inspection, which shall be sent to the Colonial Department through the Inspection of Public Works and the Governor-General of the Island; and, lastly, they shall supervise the operation, in order that this may be carried out in accordance with the stipulated conditions.

(Article 64 of the Law.)

CHAPTER III.

CONCESSIONS TO EXECUTE WITH SUBSIDY WORKS IN CHARGE OF THE STATE.

ART. 41. When a work included in the plans of the State is in question, by the method of concession to individuals or Companies, and with a subsidy in any of the manners provided in Article 73 of the general Law of Public Works, the provisions of articles 20 to 25 of these Regulations shall be observed in relation to the plans.

The investigations provided for in article 24 shall be applied in this case to the necessity of the subsidy and the amount of the same.

The project, with the schedule of rates proposed for the use and profit of the work, and the investigations which shall have been made in the proceedings, shall be then sent to the Consulting Board of Roads, Canals, and Ports, for the final decision of the Colonial Secretary concerning the approval of the plans and proceeding to draw the basis for the grant of the concession and the collection of the means specified in the schedules, as well as the special conditions as to the powers mentioned in Article 28 of these Regulations, in regard to all of which the petitioner must express his acceptance.

In the same manner the kind of subsidy, its amount, and the times and manner in which it shall be paid to the concessionaire, in accordance with what may be determined on, shall be fixed according to the nature of the works and the special laws and Regulations for their execution.

(Articles 75, 76, and 77 of the Law.)

ART. 42. When the bases of the concession have been agreed on and mutually accepted, the appraisal of the accepted project shall be made, which shall be done in the manner provided by Article 35 of the Regulations.

(Article 77 of the Law.)

ART. 43. With the facts referred to in the two preceding articles, the Colonial Secretary shall present to the Cortes the form of law for the granting of the concession.

When the law is promulgated the concession shall be offered at public auction for the period of three months. No one may take part in these auctions except those who prove that they have made the deposit of 1 per cent of the estimates as a guarantee of the fulfillment of the offers which they make. The approved estimate shall serve as the basis of the bids, which shall be made on the reduction of the amount of the subsidy.

The bidding shall be made in accordance with the existing rules, and the signer of the most advantageous proposition shall be declared the best bidder, a memorandum being made thereof, which should be submitted for the approval of the Colonial Secretary.

(Articles 77, 78, and 79 of the Law.)

ART. 44. In case of equal proposals concerning the amount of the subsidy, another bidding shall be made within the period of ten days by means of sealed bids.

In this bidding only those who have signed the propositions which appear equal shall take part, whose deposits shall be retained. This second bidding shall take place on the basis of the reduction of the schedule of rates, in the manner provided for by Article 36. If in this auction no bid whatsoever shall be made, or if there should again result an equality of the best propositions, there shall immediately be an open bidding made, based on a reduction in the time of the concession, in the manner provided for by Article 37. If the proposer should not make any bid at this open bidding, the one who shall have drawn the lowest number referred to in Article 13 of the instructions of the 18th of March, 1852,[1] shall be declared the best bidder; this drawing by lot shall be made before the same auction board referred to in the preceding article of these Regulations.

(Article 78 of the Law.)

ART. 45. The petitioner whose project shall have served as the basis for the auction, in case he shall not have been declared the best bidder, shall reserve the right of preference on equal terms, of which he may take advantage, thus declaring at the time of the bidding, in the same manner as is provided in Article 38 of these Regulations. In such case the bid shall be awarded him and the concession shall be granted to him.

If the petitioner does not take advantage of this right, the bid shall be awarded and the concession shall be granted to the best bidder; but in such case the latter shall be obliged to pay to the petitioner who presented the approved project, within the term of one month, the amount of the appraisal made in the manner provided by Article 42.

(Article 78 of the Law.)

ART. 46. When the concession is granted, the concessionaire shall deposit in the proper place the guaranty for the security of the fulfill-

---

[1] See Art. 13 of the Instructions of the 13th of February, 1852.

ment of his obligations. This guaranty shall in such case be an amount equivalent to 5 per cent of the estimate of the works included in the approved plan.

The guaranty shall be made within fifteen days, counting from the date on which the interested party is notified of the granting of the concession, for which purpose he must give a receipt which shall show the date on which such notice was given him.

If the concessionaire allows the time fixed to elapse without having deposited the guaranty, the award shall be declared without effect, the concession being again open to public bids for the period of forty days, and the interested party forfeiting the deposit of 1 per cent.

The guaranty referred to in this article shall not be returned to the concessionaire until the day when, being finished, the works shall be turned over to the public service, after the proper authorization to that effect.

(Art. 80 of the Law.)

ART. 47. No modifications can be introduced in the approved project for subsidized works without the prerequisites demanded by article 82 of the general Law of Public Works, the consequences of such variations being set forth in article 84 of the same Law.

(Articles 82 and 83 of the Law.)

ART. 48. The concession of a subsidized work shall be forfeited whenever its stipulations shall not be complied with. The forfeiture shall in such case be declared by Royal Decree issued by the Colonial Secretary, and it shall not be decreed without previous proceedings, in which the interested party shall be heard, and in which the Consulting Board of Roads, Canals, and Ports and the full Council of State shall report.

Every forfeiture shall carry with it the loss of the guaranty given by the concessionaire, to whom there remains the appeal by way of the administrative jurisdiction of contests, in order to make such claims as may be deemed proper, according to the provisions of article 87 of the general Law of Public Works.

(Articles 84 and 87 of the Law.)

ART. 49. In case of force majeure, the Colonial Secretary may grant an extension for the completion of the works, in conformity with the provisions of paragraph 2 of article 85 of the Law. In order to grant it, a second proceeding shall be necessary, which shall serve as the basis of a petition of the concessionaire, stating the reasons on which the request is founded and indicating the duration of the extension.

When the petition of the concessionaire is presented to the Governor-General of the Island, it will be sent to the governors of the provinces in which the work is to be done according to the project, and the governors will hold an investigation, in which shall be heard the Provincial Deputations, the Board of Agriculture, Industry, and Commerce of the place, where the work is situated, and the Chief Engineers of the Provinces or service to which the works belong.

There shall also be heard the officers and Corporations that the Colonial Secretary shall designate, as the case may demand.

The investigation shall deal with the facts stated by the concessionaire in his petition and the other facts which the Governor-General shall deem pertinent in connection with the matter. The Chief Engineers shall, moreover, discuss the question and state whether, in their opinion, the time requested is considered sufficient or excessive for the termination of the works which still remain to be executed.

The proceedings shall be sent by the Governor-General, with his own opinion and that of the General Inspection of Public Works, to the Colonial Secretary, who, after hearing the opinion of the Consulting Board of Roads, Canals, and Ports and the full Council of State, shall decide upon the requested extension.

In no case shall the extension be granted for a number of years greater than that which, according to the stipulations of the original conditions of the concession, shall elapse between the beginning and the termination of the works.

(Article 85 of the Law.)

ART. 50. In case the operation of the subsidized work shall be interrupted, the provisions of Article 86 of the general Law of Public Works shall be followed.

(Article 86 of the Law.)

ART. 51. When the forfeiture of a concession is declared, the Engineers of the State shall proceed, at the expense of the concessionaire, to the appraisal of the executed works, according to the provisions of Article 88 of the Law, and of Article 30 of these Regulations, concerning concessions without subsidies.

When this appraisal has been made and duly approved, the biddings referred to in Articles 88 and 89 of the said general Law shall be proceeded with, the said appraisal serving as the basis therefor, and the proceedings following the provisions of Articles 90, 91, and 92 of the same Law.

(Articles 88, 89, 90, 91, and 92 of the Law.)

ART. 52. Articles 32 and 33 of these Regulations, concerning the admission of projects for the same work and the selection by the Colonial Secretary of those which offer the greatest advantages, shall be applicable to the case of a petition for subsidized concessions. The same is true of Article 34, concerning the acceptance by the petitioners of the modifications which the superior authority may deem proper to introduce in the projects for the bases of the concession. In view of all these proceedings, there shall be declared which of the projects presented is the one which shall serve as the basis for the biddings; it being always understood that, in case of equality of all other circumstances, this declaration shall be made in favor of the project which was first presented.

(Article 78 of the Law.)

ART. 53. When the project which shall serve as the basis for the public bidding shall be determined on, the proceedings shall follow the provisions of the various articles of this chapter for cases in which there is only one project, and the signer of the one selected shall have the rights which are reserved to him by Article 45 of these Regulations.

(Article 78 of the Law.)

ART. 54. When, at the cost of the State and according to the provisions of Article 26 of the general Law of Public Works, a work shall be executed for the use and profit of which rates have been established, the operation shall be carried on by contract, in accordance with the provisions of this chapter, in so far as they may be applicable to this case.

Nevertheless when, after the proceedings prescribed by said article of the Law, it is declared convenient that the operation shall be carried on at the expense of the State, said operation shall be made by management and in accordance with the special instructions which in each case shall be given by the Colonial Secretary.

(Article 26 of the Law.)

ART. 55. Besides the supervision which the Engineers of the Government shall exercise over the execution of the works and their operation, as provided by Article 40 of these Regulations, concerning works without subsidy, said officials shall, in the cases included in this Chapter III, examine into the conditions under which the concessionaire shall receive the subsidy, so that in this connection the stipulations shall also be strictly carried out.

TITLE SECOND.

PROVINCIAL WORKS.

CHAPTER IV. ·

PROJECTS AND EXECUTION OF WORKS BY ORDINARY CONTRACTS.

ART. 56. The roads and ports for their respective territories which are of merely provincial interest, and the sanitation of lakes and marshes referred to in the third paragraph of Article 5 of the Law, are in charge of the Provinces, in accordance with Article 5 of the general Law and the special law of Public Works.

The plans of the works which are to be in charge of the corresponding Deputations shall be made as determined by the Regulations for the execution of the special law of Public Works.

(Articles 5, 9, and 33 of the Law.)

ART. 57. When the plans of the works which are to be in their charge are made by the Deputation of a Province, they shall be sent to the Colonial Department by the Governor-General, with his report, showing the reasons therefor.

His approval, if proper, shall be made by Royal Decree, published by the Colonial Secretary.

(Article 33 of the Law.)

ART. 58. When the plans of the works of the Provinces have been once approved, the order of preference fixed for them shall not be changed in the execution thereof, unless after a proposal of the Deputation assigning reasons therefor, which shall be submitted to the report of the Municipal Councils of the towns interested in the proposed works and of the Chief Engineer of the Province.

The Governor shall send the proceedings, with his report, to the Colonial Secretary, who shall decide on the proposal by means of a Royal Decree, after hearing the opinion of the Consulting Board of Roads, Canals, and Ports.

(Article 33 of the Law.)

ART. 59. Before the execution of any work included in the plan of a Province, there shall first be a resolution of the Deputation, which shall in such case order the Engineer or his assistant in charge of provincial works to proceed to the study of the respective project. This project shall follow in its draft the same formulas prescribed for the works of the State, and when it has been once finished shall pass for the report of the Chief Engineer of the Province.

When this report is made, if it should be favorable, the Deputation may approve the project, or otherwise adopt the necessary measures for its modification, in accordance with the report which may be made by the Engineer.

If the Deputation is not satisfied with the report made by the Chief Engineer, it shall send the project to the Governor-General, in order that it may be submitted to the superior authority, the Colonial Department deciding in such case by means of a Royal Decree, after hearing the opinion of the Consulting Board of Roads, Canals, and Ports.

(Article 15 of the Law.)

ART. 60. When the execution of a work of those included in the plan shall be decided on by the Deputation, and the project approved in the manner indicated by the preceding articles, the necessary credit for its execution shall be included in the provincial budget.

The work may be carried on by management or contract, which shall be decided on by the Deputation after hearing the opinion of the expert in charge of provincial works on this point.

(Articles 35 and 38 of the Law.)

ART. 61. If the works shall be executed by management, it shall be directed by the technical agents of the Deputation and in accordance with the instructions which these may give, with the approval of the provincial corporation.

If it shall be made by contract, this can not be carried out without public bidding, in accordance in all respects to what is prescribed for similar cases by the laws for the works in charge of the State, in Chapter I of these Regulations.

(Articles 38 and 39 of the Law.)

ART. 62. When a work which is not contained in any of the plans of the province is in question, and it is nevertheless deemed necessary to execute it before the above-mentioned plans, there must in all cases be first made the declaration referred to in the second paragraph of Article 35 of the general Law of Public Works.

For this declaration the proceedings to be followed, shall be started on the proposal of the Provincial Deputation made to the Governor, which must be accompanied by the project of the work in question. The Governor shall submit this proposition to the same proceedings to which the formation of plans of provincial works are subject, thereafter sending them, with his own report, to the Colonial Secretary through the Governor-General.

The proceedings shall pass for the report of the Consulting Board of Roads, Canals, and Ports, and shall finally be decided by means of a Royal Decree concerning the requested declaration.

The information above mentioned shall not be necessary when there shall have been promulgated a law authorizing the execution of the work.

In case the work be of such nature as not to correspond with those which, according to special laws, are covered by the plans of the provinces, after the investigation shall have been made, there shall be presented to the Cortes, by the Colonial Secretary, a form of decree, in order that its execution may be authorized by the legislative power.

(Article 35 of the Law.)

ART. 63. There shall precede in all cases, the concession of public domain and the declaration of public utility, to the execution of every provincial work which is not included in the respective plans, in accordance with the provisions of the general Law of Public Works, and according to the proceedings prescribed by title fourth of the present Regulations. Exception is made of the cases provided for in the previous article, when the authorization should have been or shall be granted by law.

(Article 35 of the Law.)

ART. 64. The works of repair and of preservation of the provincial works shall be carried out in accordance with the credits, which for this purpose shall be included in the budgets of the Deputation as obligatory expenses. The experts in charge of public works shall make an estimate of the repairs, approval of which shall always precede their execution, as well as the annual estimates for preservation, which shall be indispensable and sufficient for the existing works of the province which are in charge of the Deputations. The amounts calculated by the technical officials for such objects shall be necessarily included among the obligatory expenses.

(Articles 14 and 41 of the Law.)

ART. 65. When the work which is to be executed may be the subject of operation with profit, the Deputation shall make the list of rates which it considers proper to establish for its use and profit, and shall send it to the Governor of the province. The latter shall send it to the General Government with his own report, after hearing the Chief Engineer of the province, and the Governor-General, after the report of the Inspection of Public Works, shall forward it with his own to the Colonial Secretary. The approval of the establishment of rates and of the instructions for their application shall be made by means of a Royal Decree by the said Department, with the consent of the Council of Secretaries.

(Article 37 of the Law.)

ART. 66. The appointment of an expert or experts, who shall be charged with the direction of provincial works, shall be freely made by the Deputation; but this appointment shall always be of individuals who shall be Engineers of the Corps of Roads, Canals, and Ports, or at least Assistants of Public Works. In each case the salary, as well as the indemnity which shall be given to said officials for the expenses arising from the service, shall be paid from the provincial funds.

(Article 39 of the Law.)

ART. 67. In the same manner the Deputation shall have the right, in the form in which it may be deemed convenient, to organize the subordinate personnel of all kinds which may have to aid the Chief Expert in carrying out his duties, as well as the appointment of this personnel, all being at the suggestion of the said Chief.

(Article 39 of the Law.)

ART. 68. The Engineers of Roads, Canals, and Ports, who may be named by the Deputation for the direction of the service of provincial works, shall preserve all their rights under the Regulations as individuals of the Corps to which they belong, in the same manner as if they were in the service of the State.

Similar rights shall be enjoyed by the Assistants of Public Works who may be named for the same duties, and the same benefit shall inure to the overseers of the said branch who may form part of the subordinate personnel of the provincial service.

(Article 39 of the Law.)

ART. 69. The public works which are executed at the instance of the Provincial Deputation shall be executed under the inspection, in the technical branch, of the Colonial Department and the Governor-General. For this purpose the Governor may order that they be inspected during their construction by the Chief Engineer of the province, whenever he may deem this opportune.

Besides these extraordinary inspections, the Chief Engineer shall annually make other ordinary inspections of all provincial works.

The Engineer shall report the result of his inspections to the Governor of the province, and if any difficulty is noted in the works he shall so inform the latter.

The Governor, in view thereof, shall give his orders to the Deputation, in order that the difficulties may be corrected. If the Deputation should refuse to do so, or deem it proper to appeal from the decision of the Authority, the proceedings shall be carried to the Colonial Secretary, in order that he may decide the question, after first hearing the opinion of the Consulting Board of Roads, Canals, and Ports.

The Chief Engineer shall also send to the General Inspection of the Island copies of the reports sent to the Governor, informing the Inspection of all the incidents of this service.

The expenses of any kind which may be caused by the inspection of provincial works shall be charged to the corresponding Deputations.

(Article 42 of the Law.)

ART. 70. Without prejudice to the inspections referred to in the preceding article, every provincial work shall be necessarily inspected by the Chief Engineer of the Province, or by the State Engineer who may be designated for this purpose, before turning it over to public use, and when the Deputation declares that it is terminated.

For this purpose, when such case is believed to have arisen, the Deputation shall inform the Governor, who shall order that the Chief Engineer make the inspection. Said Engineer shall report to the Governor the result of his commission, and if there are any defects found, proceedings shall be instituted in accordance with the case of the preceding article, the delivery of the work to the public service being suspended until the authorization of the Governor-General or of the Colonial Secretary shall have been given.

(Article 42 of the Law.)

ART. 71. The provisions of this chapter are applicable to works called civil constructions, devoted to the service of the Colonial Department, which are in charge of the province, without any other difference than that the plans shall be gone over, when the direction or inspection shall be made, by the proper Architects in accordance with the provisions of article 39 of the general Law.

CHAPTER V.

CONCESSIONS FOR THE EXECUTION OF PROVINCIAL WORKS.

ART. 72. Every public work in charge of a province which is included in the plans of the same, can be carried out by the method of concession to individuals or corporations who may so request it, after the proceedings which are established by the general Law of Public Works and those determined by the present Regulations.

(Article 53 of the Law.)

ART. 73. The concession of every provincial work included in the approved plans, shall be granted by the corresponding Deputation, whether a subsidy of any kind has been requested for its execution, or whether in any manner whatsoever, aid from the provincial funds has been demanded.

(Articles 53 and 73 of the Law.)

ART. 74. In case the work is requested without subsidy, the petitioner shall present to the corresponding Deputation the project of the work which he desires to carry out. For this purpose he may request the Governor of the province for the authorization referred to in Article 56 of the general Law of Public Works, an authorization which, in a proper case, shall be granted with similar requisites to those referring to works of the State, as determined by Article 21 of the present Regulations.

The projects in all cases shall be drawn as provided for by Article 6.

(Articles 55 and 56 of the Law.)

ART. 75. Within the period designated by the Governor, the petitioner shall present the project to the Deputation, accompanied by a certificate which shows that he has delivered in the depository of provincial funds an amount equivalent to 1 per cent of the estimate.

The Secretary of the Deputation shall give the interested person the proper receipt, stating the day and the hour on which he received the project.

(Article 57 of the Law.)

ART. 76. The project shall be sent to the Chief of the technical service of provincial works, in order that he may go over it on the ground. The said Chief shall investigate concerning the exactness of the facts stated in the project and concerning all the technical details, making his report to the Deputation.

This corporation shall then send the project to the Chief Engineer of the Province, in order that he may make report concerning it, in the manner determined by Article 59 of these Regulations, in accordance with which the further proceedings shall follow the provisions necessary for the approval of the project by the Deputation, as if in case of a disagreement between it and the Chief Engineer.

When works in connection with ports are in question, there shall be followed, moreover, the provisions concerning the formation of plans established in the special law and determined by the Regulations for its execution.

(Article 58 of the Law.)

ART. 77. The projected schedules of rates which the petitioner proposes to establish for the use and profit of the work, shall be submitted by the Deputation to a public investigation, in which, for at least a period of ten days, there shall be heard claims of all those who consider themselves interested. After hearing the petitioner as to these claims, and lastly the Municipal Councils of the districts in which the work is to be executed, the Chief of the service of provincial works and the Chief Engineer of the province shall be heard.

When the proceedings are thus closed, the Provincial Deputation shall decide as to the granting thereof, by means of a resolution, which shall be published in the Boletin Oficial.

In this resolution, in the proper case, shall be inserted the essential conditions of the concession, which shall be those stated in the general Law of Public Works, and in Article 28, Chapter II, of these Regulations, for concessions of works in charge of the State.

From the resolution of the Deputation, in the proper case, the petitioner may appeal to the Governor-General of the Island and the Colonial Secretary, in the manner provided by the provincial law in force. (Articles 58 and 59 of the Law.)

ART. 78. When the concession is granted and the proper guaranty is given, the concessionaire shall execute the works in strict accordance with the stipulations, and under the supervision of the technical officials of the Deputation and the inspection of the State Engineers.

The concession shall be forfeited in the cases prescribed in the conditions, and shall be declared, if there be proper reason for it, by the Deputation, after previous proceedings in which shall be heard the interested party, who shall reserve the right of appeal to the Governor-General and the Colonial Secretary from the resolution of said corporation.

In case an appeal is made, the Colonial Secretary shall decide, after hearing the Consulting Board of Roads, Canals, and Ports, the concessionaire having the right to appeal from this decision by means of the administrative litigation. (Articles 8, 64, and 67 of the Law.)

ART. 79. The consequences of forfeiture and the proceedings which have to follow shall be those which are provided by Chapter II of these Regulations for similar cases in works of the State, it being understood that the appraisal of the works provided for by Article 30 shall be made by the expert agents of the Province, investigated by the Chief Engineer, and approved by the Deputation, with the right of appeal to the Government in cases of disagreement between them. (Articles 68, 69, 70, and 71 of the Law.)

ART. 80. When there shall have been presented two or more projects for the execution of the same work within the period of thirty days, counting from the time in which the first petition was presented, the comparison referred to by Article 76 and other investigations of the proceedings shall be made in connection with all the projects presented, making a note of the advantages or disadvantages of each one. In this case the Deputation shall select, for the granting of the concession, the one which, in its opinion, offers the greatest advantages. (Article 61 of the Law.)

ART. 81. In case there should result from the investigation an equality of circumstances between the projects presented, the Deputation shall resolve to proceed to a public auction on the basis of the proper project, in accordance with the provisions of Article 34 for the concession of State works.

The appraisal of the project which shall serve as the basis of the bids shall be made by two experts, one named by the Deputation and the other by the petitioner, the third being named by both parties, and, in case of disagreement, by the proper judicial authority.

The appraisal shall be made on the basis designated by Article 35, and shall be submitted for the approval of the Deputation, which shall decide, after first hearing the expert in charge of provincial works.

(Article 62 of the Law.)

ART. 82. The bidding shall take place before the Deputation and shall follow the similar rules established for this purpose in articles 36 and 37, the President of the Board having the right to declare who is the best bidder, saving the approval of the said Corporation.

The author of the project which shall serve as the basis of the bidding reserves the right of preference on equal terms, and that of receiving the value of his project, according to the appraisal, in a similar manner to the provisions of Articles 38 and 39 of these Regulations.

(Articles 62 and 72 of the Law.)

ART. 83. When an individual or a company asks for the concession of a work included in one of the plans of the province, with subsidy or aid from the funds of the same, in so far as the presentation, proceedings, and approval of the project are concerned, the provisions of Articles 74, 75, and 76 of these Regulations shall be observed; and concerning the schedules for the use and benefit of the work, it shall be subject to the investigation prescribed by Article 77.

Thereafter the appraisal of the project shall be made, which shall be carried out as provided for this purpose by the rules established in Article 81.

(Articles 75 and 76 of the Law.)

ART. 84. In the case in which the Deputation shall have approved the project, the rates, and other documents of the proceedings, and provided that the petitioner accept the modifications which it may have been deemed convenient to introduce into them by reason of the result of the investigations, there shall follow the granting of the concession which is within the power of a provincial Corporation after public bidding, at which the approved project shall serve as the basis, and which shall take place before said Corporation, in a manner similar to that provided in articles 43 and 44 for the cases of works of the State.

In the same case the author of the proposal whose project shall have served as the basis of the bids, has the right of preference on equal terms and to the payment of said project, in accordance with provisions similar to those set forth in article 45.

(Articles 77, 78, and 79 of the Law.)

ART. 85. The guaranty shall be deposited in the depository of the Deputation, following in all respects the provisions of article 46 of these Regulations on this point.

Article 47, concerning modifications in projects, and article 48, concerning forfeitures, which in this case shall be declared by the Deputations in the form and with the same rights of appeal as those set forth in the second paragraph of article 78, and the provisions of article 79, are also applicable to concessions subsidized with provincial funds.

Article 49, concerning extension for the termination of the works, and article 50, concerning the interruption of the operation, are also applicable to the case referred to in the present article.

(Articles 80, 82, 83, 84, 85, 86, 87, 88, 89, 90, 91, and 92 of the Law.)

ART. 86. When there shall have been presented two or more propositions to execute a provincial work with subsidy, within the time expressed by Article 80, the provisions of said article shall be applied for the selection of the project which shall serve as the basis of the bids, proceeding to the appraisal of said project, and thereafter following, for the carrying out of the bidding and subsequent proceedings, the rules established in Article 82 of these Regulations.

(Article 78 of the Law.)

ART. 87. When there shall have been executed at the expense of the Deputation a work which may be the subject of a profitable operation, this operation shall be carried on by contract, the concession thereof being awarded to the best bidder. The bidding shall take place in all respects in accordance with the provisions of this chapter for concessions of works without subsidy; and there shall serve as a basis for the bidding the schedule of rates made by the Deputation and approved in the manner indicated by Article 65.

If the provincial Deputation should request the operation referred to in this article, the proper proceedings shall be instituted, in which the Chief Engineer, the Governor of the Province, the Inspector of Public Works, and the Consulting Board of Roads, Canals, and Ports shall report concerning the propriety of the petition, in view of which the Colonial Secretary shall decide what he may deem proper.

(Article 37 of the Law.)

ART. 88. The officials or technical employees of the Deputation shall carry out the duties which belong to them for the works which are executed and operated in accordance with the stipulated conditions, and shall exercise the proper supervision, in order that the concessionaire shall not receive the subsidy, except at the times and in the manner provided for by the conditions.

(Article 81 of the Law.)

ART. 89. The Colonial Secretary shall have the final decision concerning the approval of projects, granting of concessions, declarations of forfeiture, and, in general, concerning all the proceedings relative to the provisions of the General Law of Public Works and of these Regulations, which belong to the Provincial Deputations when the works include two or more provinces and the Deputations of the said provinces do not agree.

(Articles 8 and 15 of the Law and chapters 6 and 7 of the same.)

ART. 90. The provisions contained in chapters 2 and 3, which refer to concessions of works of the State, and which have not been expressly mentioned in the present chapter, shall be applicable to concessions of provincial works, with the modifications required by the various cases, the questions which may arise in this connection concerning the application of these Regulations being decided according to the spirit of said provisions.

(Article 5 of the Law.)

TITLE THIRD.

MUNICIPAL WORKS.

CHAPTER VI.

PROJECTS AND EXECUTION OF WORKS BY ORDINARY CONTRACT.

ART. 91. Local roads, the supply of water, local ports, and the drainage of lakes and marshes of merely municipal interest are in charge of the Municipal Councils, in accordance with Article 6 of the general Law and the special laws of Public Works.

The plans of the works of the Municipal Councils shall be made in accordance with the provisions of the Regulations for the execution of the special laws of Public Works.

(Articles 6, 10, and 43 of the Law.)

ART. 92. The order of preference stated in the plan of the Municipal Council for the execution of the work can not be changed except by virtue of a proposal, giving reasons therefor, by the Municipality, which shall be duly approved by the Governor, after hearing the Provincial Deputation and the Chief Engineer.

(Article 43 of the Law.)

ART. 93. When a Municipal Council decides on the execution of a work included in the plan of the Municipality, the proper project shall first of all be made. This project shall be drawn in accordance with the terms then in force, and once drawn shall be presented to the Governor for approval, who shall grant it only after hearing the Chief Engineer of the Province.

The Governor, when works of great importance are in question, or when he is not satisfied with the opinion of the Chief Engineer, shall submit the project for the approval of the Colonial Secretary, who shall, before granting it, hear the Consulting Board of Roads, Canals, and Ports.

After the project is approved, the Municipal Council shall include in the Municipal budget the corresponding credit to carry out the work.

(Articles 17 and 43 of the Law.)

ART. 94. After the project of a municipal work has been approved, and the proper credit incorporated in the budget, its execution shall be proceeded with by the method of management or contract, as shall be decided on by the Municipal Council after hearing the expert who shall have drawn the plan.

If the work shall be carried out by management, it shall be directed by said expert, in accordance with the instructions in force for municipal works. In case it shall be done by contract, the public bidding in the manner analogous to what is prescribed by these regulations for the works of the State and of a Province, is an indispensable prerequisite.

(Article 47 of the Law.)

ART. 95. When a work not included in the plan of a Municipality is in question, there shall first of all be made the project by the expert to whom the Municipal Council shall have deemed it convenient to intrust this work.

When the project is drawn it shall be submitted to a public investigation, at which shall be heard, within the time which for this purpose is designated by the Municipal Council, all individuals who desire to make any claim concerning the propriety of the execution of the work.

After this investigation is had, the Municipal Council shall send the proceedings to the Governor with its report concerning said claims, and said authority shall decide what may be deemed expedient, after hearing the opinions of the Provincial Deputation and the Chief Engineer. When the nature of the work requires it he shall also hear the Marine Authority or the Military Authority, the Provincial Board of Health, and the Board of Agriculture, Industry, and Commerce, as the case may be.

From the decision of the Governor the Municipal Council may appeal to the Governor General and the Colonial Secretary, who, after hearing the Consulting Board of Roads, Canals, and Ports, shall decide without further recourse.

(Article 45 of the Law.)

ART. 96. When a work which is to be executed affects two or more Municipal Councils, the decision concerning the proposal of preference indicated by Article 92, or the approval of the project referred to in Article 93, or the other points indicated in Articles 94 and 95, can not be made, unless the interested Municipal Councils shall have come to an agreement, and unless they have before them the complete project.

If there should be any difference of opinion between the said Municipal Councils, the Governor shall decide after hearing the Chief Engineer and the Provincial Deputation, the Municipality which may have considered itself prejudiced having the right of appeal to the Governor General and the Colonial Secretary. When the works affect towns belonging to different provinces, the proceeding shall be according to the last paragraph of Article 46 of the General Law of Public Works.

(Article 45 of the Law.)

ART. 97. For the construction of public works of any kind, Municipal Councils may call for the personal aid of the inhabitants whenever the ordinary revenues, or any other income devoted to such objects, shall not be sufficient.

ART. 98. "Municipal Councils may impose special taxes for the use and profit of the works which are executed and which are the subject of profitable operation. The amount of taxes shall be proposed by the Municipality in each particular case, submitting its proposal to the Governor, who, with his report, shall submit it to the Governor-General, and the latter, with his report, to the Colonial Secretary, who shall decide, by Royal Order, after hearing the Colonial Department of the Council of State, concerning the approval of the proposed tax, communicating the proper instructions for its application to the work in question.

(Article 46 of the Law.)

ART. 99. The work of preservation and repair of existing works in each Municipality shall be paid by the credits previously and necessarily designated for this purpose in the municipal budget, and always after these budgets have been drawn and approved by the proper Municipal Council.

(Articles 16 and 49 of the Law.)

ART. 100. The Municipal Councils may freely name the technical officials who are to intervene in the works under their charge, it being necessary that those selected shall have the proper professional degree which proves their ability.

The organization of the technical personnel, the management of municipal works, the fixing of the payments, and other matters relative to this part of the service shall be exercised by the proper Municipal Council, in accordance with the provisions of the laws and regulations in force.

Engineers of Roads and Overseers of Public Works who may be named by the Municipal Councils for the service of municipal works shall enjoy all the rights which are given them by the Regulations, as though they were in the service of the State.

(Article 48 of the Law.)

ART. 101. Public works in charge of Municipal Councils shall be inspected by the employees or technical officials of the State in a manner similar to that prescribed by articles 69 and 70 of the present Regulations for provincial works.

(Articles 8 and 50 of the Law.)

ART. 102. The provisions of this chapter are applicable to works called civil constructions devoted to municipal services, and which may be in charge of Municipal Councils, without any other difference than that of the experts in whose charge shall be the projects, direction, and supervision, according to existing legislation.

(Article 48 of the Law.)

CHAPTER VII.

CONCESSIONS OF MUNICIPAL WORKS.

ART. 103. The public works in charge of Municipal Councils which are included in the plans of the same, properly approved, can be the subject of concessions to individuals or Companies who may request them, in accordance with the provisions of the general Law of Public Works and of the present Regulations.

(Article 53 of the Law.)

ART. 104. The concessions to which the previous article refers shall be granted by the proper Municipal Councils, provided that no aid of any kind whatsoever is requested for them, nor any subsidy from the Municipal funds.

(Articles 53 and 73 of the Law.)

ART. 105. Whenever a concession of a municipal work without subsidy is requested, the petitioner shall present to the proper Municipal Council the project of the same. For this purpose he may request the Governor of the province to give the authorization referred to in Article 56 of the general Law of Public Works, proceeding as prescribed by Article 74 of these Regulations concerning provincial works.

(Articles 55 and 56 of the Law.)

ART. 106. The project shall be delivered to the Secretary of the Municipal Council, accompanied by a document which proves that the petitioner has delivered to the depository of municipal funds a sum equivalent to 1 per cent of the estimate of the works. The Secretary of the Municipal Council shall give a receipt for the project, in which shall appear the day and the hour on which it was presented.

(Article 57 of the Law.)

ART. 107. The expert in charge of municipal works, or the one whom the Municipal Council deemed proper to temporarily name for this special purpose, shall then proceed to go over the plan of the project on the ground and report in the manner provided for by Article 76 for provincial works. The Municipal Council shall send the project thus reported to the Governor of the province, who, after hearing the Chief Engineer, shall decide as to the approval of the project, in the manner prescribed by Article 96.

(Article 58 of the Law.)

ART. 108. The schedule of rates for the use and profit of the work shall be submitted for a period of fifteen days to a public investigation, under the direction of the Alcalde, in which all the inhabitants of the town who believe themselves interested may enter claims. The Alcalde shall then send this investigation to the petitioner, in order that he may answer; and shall further hear the expert in charge, and, with the opinion of the full Municipal Council, shall send the proceedings to the Governor. The latter shall decide concerning the approval of the rates in the same manner as is provided for the project by the preceding article.

(Article 58 of the Law.)

ART. 109. After the project is approved and the basis of the contract agreed upon with the petitioner, the Municipal Council shall decide as to the granting of the concession by means of a resolution, in which a memorandum shall be made and which shall be communicated to the Governor for publication in the Boletin Oficial.

The essential provisions of these concessions shall be those provided by Article 28 of these Regulations for similar concessions of works of the State.

From the resolution of the Municipal Council the petitioner may appeal to the Governor, who, after hearing the Provincial Deputation, shall decide without further recourse. The periods for investigation and decision, and the form in which the appeal shall be made, are those designated for these cases by the Municipal Law in force in this island.

(Articles 58 and 59 of the Law.)

ART. 110. When the concession is granted, the concessionaire shall deposit from 3 to 5 per cent of the amount of the approved estimate, and proceed to the execution of the works under the immediate inspection of the technical officials of the Municipality, and the superior inspection of the State Engineers.

(Articles 50, 59, and 64 of the Law.)

ART. 111. The concession shall be forfeited in the cases provided in the stipulated provisions, and shall thus be declared in a proper case by the Municipal Council, after proceedings in which the interested party shall be heard, and with a right of appeal to the Governor in the same manner as is provided for in Article 109.

After the Governmental proceedings have been exhausted, the concessionaire shall reserve the right to appeal from the declaration of forfeiture of the concession, by administrative litigation.

When the forfeiture is finally declared, the consequences shall be the same as those provided for by chapter 2 of these Regulations for similar works in charge of the State, it being understood that the appraisal of the works executed, to which Article 30 refers, shall be made by the expert employees of the Municipal Council, the approval of the Governor being necessary in the same manner as for projects of municipal works.

(Articles 67, 68, 69, 70, and 71 of the Law.)

ART. 112. In case more than one project is presented for the same work within a period of thirty days, counting from the time the first petition is made, the comparison on the ground, referred to by Article 107, and other investigations of the proceedings, shall be made by comparison between the projects presented, discussing their respective advantages and disadvantages. When these proceedings are ended the Municipal Council, in view of the result, shall select the project which, in its judgment, offers the greatest advantages, and send it for the approval of the Governor.

The Governor, having in view all the proceedings, after an opinion of the Chief Engineer, shall decide upon the approval in the manner determined by Article 93.

From the decision of the Governor, the Municipal Council, if it deems it proper, may appeal to the Governor-General and the Colonial Secretary, who shall decide without further recourse.

(Article 61 of the Law.)

ART. 113. If evident advantages appear in one of the projects over the rest, this one shall be preferred for the granting of the concession, which shall be made by the Municipal Council in accordance with the provisions of Article 109.

If it appears that none of the projects presented offers advantages over another, the Governor shall thus declare; and if the Municipal Council does not appeal from this ruling, he shall decide that a public bidding be held, on the basis of the project which has the priority.

Before announcing the bidding, the said project shall be appraised by an expert named by the Municipal Council and another by the petitioner, who, in their turn and before the appraisal, shall name a third by agreement, to act in case of disagreement. If there should not be an agreement between said two experts on the appointment of a third, he shall be named by the proper judicial authority.

The appraisal shall be made in a manner similar to that designated by Article 35, and the Municipal Council shall give its approval thereto, after the report of the expert in charge.

(Articles 61 and 62 of the Law.)

ART. 114. The bidding shall take place with the Alcalde presiding, assisted by the Technical Director, the Treasurer of the Municipal Council and the Secretary of the same, and in accordance with the provisions of Articles 36 and 37.

The concession shall be granted by the Municipal Council to the person who shall be declared the best bidder at the public sale, reserving to the author of the project which has served as its basis, the rights of preference on equal terms and of payment of the appraised value of the project, according to the rules established in Articles 38 and 39.

(Articles 62 and 72 of the Law.)

ART. 115. When, for the execution of a municipal work a subsidized concession is requested, to be paid from the funds of the Municipal Council, so far as presentation, proceedings and approval of the project and investigation concerning rates are concerned, the same method shall be followed as is provided by Articles 105 to 107 of this chapter referring to works without subsidy.

When the project is approved, its appraisal shall be made in the manner prescribed by Article 113.

(Article 75 and 76 of the Law.)

ART. 116. When the project is approved and the basis of the concession agreed upon between the Municipal Council and the petitioner with the approval of the Governor, the public bidding shall be had, at which the said project shall serve as the basis in a manner similar to that provided for works of the State, by Articles 43 and 44 of these Regulations.

The author of the project always has a right of preference on equal terms and to the payment of the appraisal in accordance with the provisions of Article 45.

(Article 78 and 79 of the Law.)

ART. 117. The guaranty which, in case of subsidy, shall be 5 per cent of the amount of the estimate, shall be deposited with the Treasurer of the Municipal Council.

Articles 47 to 50 of the present Regulations, with the corresponding modifications according to the provisions of Article 111, are applicable to this case.

(Article 80 of the Law.)

ART. 118. If there should be more than one project for the subsidized concession of a municipal work, the one offering the greatest advantages shall be selected, which shall serve as the basis for the bidding; and if it is believed that all the projects presented are equal, the one having priority shall serve for this object. When the project which shall serve as the basis for the bidding shall be determined, in one way or another, the appraisal shall be previously made; and for the rest there shall be applicable in this case, the same provisions which for similar cases are prescribed by the present Regulations in Article 112, and in those referring to works of the State and of the Province.

(Article 61 of the Law.)

ART. 119. When a work which shall be executed with municipal funds may be the subject of profitable operation, and the plan of rates for its use and profit shall have been approved in the manner prescribed by Article 98, such operation shall be carried out by contract, after public bidding, which shall take place according to provisions similar to those indicated by Article 36, for works of the State without subsidy.

The Municipal Council can not take charge of the operation of this class of work without previous authorization from the Government, and with formalities similar to those established by Article 87 for provincial works.

(Article 46 of the Law.)

ART. 120. When works, the concession of which is requested, affect the territory of two or more Municipal Councils of the same provinces, proceedings shall be had in each one of them independently, as to the examination of the projects and the investigations referred to in this chapter, sending the proceedings to the Governor through the respective Alcaldes.

The Governor shall decide concerning the approval of the projects as provided for by this chapter.

After the granting of concessions, declaration of forfeiture, and other resolutions which may be made by Municipal Councils, they shall come to some agreement; and if they should not be able to do so, the Governor shall decide, with a right of appeal to the Governor-General and the Colonial Secretary, and a further appeal by means of administrative litigation.

When the Municipal Councils interested belong to different provinces, the rights which according to this chapter belong to the Governors and the Municipalities, shall be exercised by the Governor-General and the Colonial Secretary, whenever the said authorities or Corporations do not agree.

(Articles 8 and 16 of the Law, and Chapters 6 and 7 of the same.)

ART. 121. The provisions of Chapters 2 and 3, of which no special mention has been made here, are applicable to concessions of municipal works with the modifications which the various cases require, the doubts and questions which may arise being decided according to the spirit of these provisions.

TITLE FOURTH.

CONCESSIONS OF WORKS NOT INCLUDED IN PLANS OF THE STATE, OF THE PROVINCE, AND OF MUNICIPAL COUNCILS.

CHAPTER VIII.

CONCESSIONS OF THE PUBLIC DOMAIN.

ART. 122. When individuals or Companies ask for the execution of public works which are not included in the plans formed by the State, the Province, and the Municipalities prior to the granting of the concession, there shall be the grant of the public domain which may be affected by the work, and the declaration of the public utility thereof.

The concession of the public domain in every case must be given by the Colonial Department or its Delegates.

If the work, the concession of which is requested, should alter in any manner the plans referred to by the preceding paragraph, the provisions of the second paragraph of Article 53 of the general Law of Public Works shall also be observed.

(Article 93 of the Law.)

ART. 123. In the concession of works which affect the public domain, the following cases are distinguished:

First. That the work in question does not hinder or impede the enjoyment or general use of the part of the public domain which it affects.

Second. That it hinders or impedes the said general use.

Third. That it permanently occupies a part of the public domain in which there is no use or general benefit.

Fourth. That it temporarily occupies a part of the public domain devoted to general use.

Fifth. That it alters established servitudes on private property for the benefit of the public domain.

(Article 94 of the Law.)

ART. 124. The person requesting the concession of a work affecting the public domain, in the manner designated in the first number of the preceding article, shall present his petition to the Colonial Secretary or to the Governor-General of the Island, accompanied with a project based on the following documents:

First. An explanatory memorial, in which a clear idea is given of the work, the execution of which is requested, and in which it is shown that neither by it nor by its operation the general use of the part of the public domain, which may be affected by said work, shall be impaired.

Second. Plans which show the situation, principal dimensions, and the other details of the work.

Third. An approximate estimate, in which, besides the calculation of the cost of the same, shall appear the value of the part of the public domain affected.

And fourth. The rates which it is proposed to establish for the use and profit of the work.

The petitioner shall accompany with the project a document showing that he has deposited in the Government Treasury an amount equal to one-half of one per cent of the estimate of the works which shall be built on lands of the public domain.

(Article 94 of the Law.)

ART. 125. The Colonial Secretary shall examine into the investigations to clear up the rights established on the public domain which it is proposed to occupy, the advantages or disadvantages which might result to the public interests from the work, and the other circumstances which it may be advisable to take into account before the granting of the concession.

These investigations shall be proceeded with in accordance with the provisions prescribed by the Regulations for the execution of the special laws of Public Works, the opinion of the Deputation being in all cases indispensable, as also that of the Chief Engineer and of the Governor of the province interested in the construction of the work, of the Inspection-General of Public Works, of the Governor-General of the Island, besides that of the Consulting Board of Roads, Canals, and Ports.

(Article 94 of the Law.)

ART. 126. The concession, if it shall be proper, shall be made by Royal Decree, except in the case that the work shall alter some of the plans of the State, according to the provisions of the second paragraph of Article 122 of these Regulations. In the concession there shall be stipulated the clauses and conditions which are set forth in Article 95 of the general Law of Public Works, and besides, the times and terms in which the State shall be paid the price at which the part of the public domain it is to cede shall be valued.

The guaranty which it is necessary for the concessionaire to give shall be 3 per cent of the estimate of the works which shall occupy the public domain, and shall be returned when he has proved that he has completed the works, as provided for by Article 103 of the general Law of Public Works.

The conditions of forfeiture in these cases shall be the same as those for concessions without subsidy established by chapter 2 of these Regulations.

(Article 95 of the Law.)

ART. 127. In the case in which, according to the provisions of Article 96 of the general Law of Public Works, more than one petition for the same work is presented, the investigations referred to in Article 125 shall cover, moreover, the question of the advantages or disadvantages which might result by a comparison between the competing projects; and the one shall be preferred which offers the greatest advantages, or, in case of equality, the first one which shall have been presented.

Thirty days shall be declared to be the time within which propositions for the execution of the work may be presented counting from the publication of the first petition. After this period has elapsed no other new petition shall be admitted.

(Article 96 of the Law.)

ART. 128. The Colonial Secretary, nevertheless, in cases where there is not a marked preference between the proposals, or in any other case in which he may deem it convenient to the general interests, may order that the concession be made by means of public bids. In this bidding not only the proposers who have presented their projects may take part, but also any person who shall have made the deposit of one-half of 1 per cent provided by article 124.

(Article 96 of the Law.)

ART. 129. For the bidding, the project which shall first have been presented shall serve as the basis, provided that its author shall have accepted the modifications which the superior authorities may have deemed proper to introduce therein. In case of failure to accept these, the deposit and the project shall be returned, and the second project shall be taken up, proceeding with it in the same manner, and thus successively until the last, it being understood that no concession shall be granted if none of the petitioners accept the modifications introduced.

(Article 96 of the Law.)

ART. 130. The project which, according to the previous article, shall serve as the basis for the bidding, shall be appraised prior thereto in the manner provided by article 50 of these Regulations.

(Article 96 of the Law.)

ART. 131. The bidding shall be made, in the first place, upon the percentage of reduction in the rates approved for the use of the works;

and in case there are equal propositions, a new open bidding shall be held between the signers of the propositions, which shall be based on the raising of the price which has been assigned to the part of the public domain which should be necessary to grant.

If the bidders should make any proposition concerning this betterment, the one who shall have drawn the lowest number by lot before proceeding to the opening of the bids, shall be declared the best bidder. (Article 96 of the Law.)

ART. 132. The petitioner to whom belongs the project which has served as the basis of the bidding, shall have the right of preference on equal terms if he so declares at the time of the public sale, which shall be extended for one-half hour for this purpose, so that he may make use of this right, which shall appear in the minutes. If he should not do so, the person who shall be declared the best bidder in the public sale shall be considered the concessionaire, by means of a declaration made by Royal Decree, issued by the Colonial Department after the deposit of a guaranty equivalent to 3 per cent of the amount of the estimate of the works affecting the public domain.

The one to whom the award is made shall, moreover, pay the petitioner whose project has served as the basis of the public sale the amount of said project, in accordance with the appraisal made, as provided by article 130. (Article 96 of the Law.)

ART. 133. The concessionaire shall pay to the State the value at which the part of the public domain which has to be granted has been fixed. This payment shall be made at the times and in the manner determined by the provisions of the concession. (Article 96 of the Law.)

ART. 134. When a work included in number 2 of article 123 of these Regulations is in question, the petitioner for the concession shall present the project referred to in article 124.

The memorial shall show the necessity for the occupation of the public domain, showing besides in what manner and to what extent the work will affect the general use established thereon.

In the proposal, besides the value of the part of the domain which is to be occupied, the damage to the general use caused by the execution of the work shall be stated, including both in a single amount.

With the project shall be accompanied the receipt for the deposit of an amount equivalent to 1 per cent of the estimate of the works which shall have to be established on lands of the public domain. (Article 94 of the Law.)

ART. 135. After the project is presented, it shall be submitted to the investigations laid down by article 125, the Colonial Secretary having the right to approve it. If the work changes the plans of the State, there shall be presented to the Cortes the proper form of law, in the manner prescribed by article 53 of the general Law of Public Works.

In every case the concession for a work of this class can not be granted without public bidding, as determined by article 97 of the same law. (Articles 94 and 97 of the Law.)

ART. 136. At the bidding the project approved shall serve as the basis, and the proposals shall be made in the first instance on reductions in the rates for the use of the work, and in case of equal propositions, on the raising of the value of the public domain which shall have to be granted, according to the figure which, for this purpose, shall have been fixed in the approved estimate, as provided in article 134. (Article 97 of the Law.)

ART. 137. The concessions shall be granted to the best bidder by means of a Royal Decree, in which shall be fixed the clauses and conditions indicated in Article 126, and the times and manner in which the concessionaire shall pay to the State the amount which shall have been fixed for the value of the part of the public domain occupied, and the damages for the loss of its general use.

The guaranty shall be 5 per cent of the estimate of the works which shall be executed on lands of public domain, and shall not be returned until the concessionaire shall have shown that he has completed the works of the concession, as provided by Article 103 of the general Law of Public Works.

The conditions of forfeiture shall be the same as those established by said Article 126 of these Regulations. (Article 98 of the Law.)

ART. 138. Whenever for the same work two or more petitions for concessions are presented, the selection of the project which is to serve as the basis of the biddings shall be proceeded with in accordance with the provisions of Articles 127 and 129, as the case may be, observing for all other purposes the provisions of Articles 130, 131, and 132. (Article 99 of the Law.)

ART. 139. The concessions referred to in the previous articles of this chapter are subject, as to their terms and their general provisions, the formalities of the grant, the right of alienation on the part of the concessionaire, the supervision of the works, and the cases of forfeiture, to the provisions established for each of these points in Articles 100 to 104, both inclusive, of the general Law of Public Works. (Articles 100 and 104 of the Law.)

ART. 140. When the work, the concession of which is demanded, is included in case number 3 of Article 123, and in consequence part of the public domain which will be affected is not devoted to any use or benefit whatever, the petitioner shall present the project drawn according to the following conditions:

First. A memorial in which the object of the work is stated, and the part of the public domain which is to be occupied, and proof that said part is not devoted to any general use.

Second. Plans which give a clear idea of the dispositions of the works.

Third. Approximate estimate of the same.

There shall be accompanied, besides, the rates which shall be established for the use of the work and the bases for their application.

(Article 106 of the Law.)

ART. 141. The project shall thereafter be the subject of an investigation, at which all the officials or Corporations shall be heard that in each case may be designated by the special laws of Public Works and the Regulations for their execution; and among them there shall always be consulted the Chief Engineer of the province and the Governor, who shall be the one to direct the investigation and who shall send its result to the General Government, which will forward it to the Colonial Department.

The Secretary, by means of a Royal Order, shall decide as to the concession, after hearing the Consulting Board of Roads.

(Article 105 of the Law.)

ART. 142. In case more than one petition for the same work is presented, all shall be submitted to a competitive examination during the investigations referred to in the preceding article; and the one shall be selected from among them which offers the greatest advantages to the public interests; and in case of equality among them the one which has been first presented; and in neither of these cases shall the other petitioners have any right of indemnity whatsoever.

(Article 105 of the Law.)

ART. 143. The essential clauses of the concessions referred to by Article 140 and the following articles shall be:

First. The guaranty which the concessionaire shall give in security for the fulfillment of his obligations. This shall not exceed one per cent of the estimate of the works affecting the public domain, and shall be returned to the interested party when the works have been executed to the value of one-third part of said estimate.

Second. The dates on which the works are to begin and end.

Third. The term of the concession, which may be perpetual in cases in which the special laws of Public Works shall so provide.

(Article 105 of the Law.)

ART. 144. These concessions shall be forfeited when the stipulated conditions shall not be fulfilled, and then shall follow proceedings similar to those provided by chapter 2, title first, of these Regulations, concerning the concessions of works of the State without subsidy.

(Article 105 of the Law.)

ART. 145. When the work which is to be executed comes within the case of number 4 of article 123, the petitioner may state his desires in a petition directed to the Governor of the province, who, following the procedure determined by the Regulations of the Special Laws, and after hearing the Chief Engineer, shall decide concerning the authorization requested, imposing the proper conditions for the enjoyment of the concession. From the decision of the Governor the interested party shall have the right of appeal to the Governor-General and to the Colonial Secretary, who shall decide finally.

By means of similar proceedings á request included in paragraph 5 of article 123 of the Regulations shall be decided, provided that the concession be temporary; but in case a perpetual concession be requested, the decision shall be made by the said Colonial Department. (Articles 107 and 108 of the Law.)

Art. 146. Grants of the public domain may be made for works devoted to the carrying on of a private industry, in accordance with article 109 of the Law. The Special Law of Public Works and the Regulations for its execution show the proceedings which in each case shall be followed in order to obtain the concession which it is proper to grant, the clauses which it shall contain, and the intervention in this matter belonging to the administrative officials. (Article 109 of the Law.)

Art. 147. If, in accordance with Article 110 of the General Law, it is requested that a company or an individual be given the concession of part of the domain of the State, for the construction of a work devoted to public or private use, the same proceedings shall be observed as are prescribed in the present chapter for the granting of the public domain; but, nevertheless, the following provisions shall be kept in mind:

First. In this case the concession shall always be made after public bidding, which shall be based on a price better than that approved in the estimate, as affects that part of the domain of the State which is to be granted.

Second. This public bidding shall take place in accordance with the proceedings and the requisites established by the laws and instructions in force for the alienation of public lands, and the amount of the public sale shall be paid in the manner provided in the same legislation.

Third. In order to take part in the bidding, a deposit of 1 per cent of the amount of the estimate of the works shall be made, and the guaranty shall be 5 per cent of the same estimate, which shall not be returned until the complete termination of the works; and

Fourth. In case of the forfeiture of the concession, the concessionaire shall lose the guaranty and the amounts which he may have paid for the value of the granted domain, the State taking charge thereof for the use which it may deem proper. (Article 110 of the Law.)

Art. 148. If the work which is to be executed changes servitudes established for the benefit of the public domain of the State, the concession thereof shall be granted by the Colonial Department or the Governors, according to whether it is perpetual or temporary, and in accordance with the proceedings provided for by Article 145 of the present Regulations. (Article 111 of the Law.)

CHAPTER IX.

DECLARATION OF PUBLIC UTILITY.

ART. 149. The declaration of public utility of the work petitioned for, shall precede the execution of all public works, the concession of which is requested by individuals or Companies, in the cases which are not excepted by Article 113 of the General Law of Public Works.

(Article 113 of the Law.)

ART. 150. In all petitions for the declaration of public utility two cases shall be distinguished; that is to say:

First. That there is not asked in any grant the benefit of neighborhood, referred to in the first paragraph of Article 114 of the General Law.

Second. That, in addition, condemnation of private property under the laws of eminent domain is requested for the benefit of the projected work.

(Article 114 of the Law.)

ART. 151. In the first case of the preceding article, the petitioner shall present a preliminary project, which shall serve as the basis for an investigation, in the manner prescribed by the following articles; this preliminary project shall contain an explanatory memorial, general plans of the works, and an idea of its cost.

(Article 116 of the Law.)

ART. 152. If the work should be of a municipal character and should be included within one single district, the preliminary plans shall be submitted to a public investigation for a period of fifteen days, the Municipal Council having the right to declare the utility, in view of the result of this investigation.

If the work, being of a municipal character, affects more than one town, the information shall be made in all those which may be interested; and thereafter each Municipal Council, by means of its respective Alcalde, shall send the proceedings to the Provincial Deputation, which, in this case, shall have the right to make the declaration of utility.

(Articles 115 and 116 of the Law.)

ART. 153. If the work should be of a provincial character and affect one province only, the preliminary project shall be submitted to an investigation of the interested Municipal Councils, and in view of these the Provincial Deputation shall decide concerning the declaration.

In the same case when the work is provincial and affects more than one province, there shall be made in each one the corresponding investigation, submitting the preliminary project to the examination of the Municipal Councils. The respective Alcaldes shall send the proceedings to the Governor, and the said Authority, after hearing the Deputation and with his own report, shall send the proceedings to the

Governor-General, who shall decide as to the declaration in view of the investigations made, when it shall be according to the Law.

(Articles 115 and 117 of the Law.)

ART. 154. In case the work should affect general interests and, as a consequence, the character of a State work, the investigation on the basis of the preliminary plan shall begin by hearing the interested Municipal Councils, thereafter the Provincial Deputation or Deputations which the work affects, and the respective Governor shall send to the Governor-General the proceedings, so that he, when the decision does not belong to him, according to Article 115 of the Law, shall send it with his report to the Colonial Secretary, who shall make the declaration by Royal Decree, according to the provisions of said article.

(Articles 115 and 117 of the Law.)

ART. 155. When the declaration of public utility shall come within the second case of Article 150, and it shall be desired to have a right of condemnation of private property under the laws of eminent domain, the petitioner shall draw the project in accordance with the provisions determined by Article 6 of these Regulations for works of the State, adding the amount of the tax and the calculation of the probable earnings of the Company.

The petitioner shall also present the documents which he may deem proper in order to prove the necessity of the declaration of utility, and shall add to the project a statement, according to the municipal districts, of all the proprietors whose estates shall have to be occupied by the execution of the work.

The project shall be delivered by the petitioner to the Governor of the province, who shall have charge of directing the investigation which is to precede the declaration.

(Articles 115 and 117 of the Law.)

ART. 156. If the work should be of a municipal character, the Governor-General shall announce in the Boletin Oficial the petition, together with the list of names of the parties interested in the condemnations, ordering at the same time that the petitioner proceed to a survey of the works on the ground, of which he shall notify the Alcalde of the district in which the work is to be executed, to the end that he give notice to the interested owners and inform them of the day or days the said survey is to take place.

The petitioner or his delegate shall then proceed, on the days fixed, to the said survey, hearing on the ground the owners of the estates which the works will have to occupy, and giving orally such explanations as they may desire.

Within twenty days following the termination of the survey the parties interested in the condemnation proceedings may make whatever claims they may deem pertinent as to their rights and shall direct the same to the Alcalde of the proper town.

The Municipal Council, after hearing the technical Director of the Municipal Works, shall deliberate concerning the claims presented, and as to whether the utility should or should not be declared; and the Alcalde shall send to the Governor-General the proceedings, with the report which might have been agreed upon by the Municipal Council, or with his own report.

The Governor, after first hearing the petitioner and the report of the Chief Engineer and of the Provincial Deputation, shall make the declaration of public utility by a resolution, setting forth the reasons, which shall be inserted in the Boletin Oficial of the Province.

(Articles 115 and 117 of the Law.)

ART. 158. If the work should be of a provisional character, the Governor shall follow all the proceedings provided for by article 156, and shall decide on the declaration, after hearing the Provincial Deputation, the petitioner, and the Chief Engineer.

If the work should be of a provisional character, affecting the territories of two or more provinces, there shall be observed in all the provinces rules similar to the preceding ones; but the Governors, instead of deciding, shall confine themselves to sending, with their report to the Governor-General, the investigations made in their respective provinces. The Governor-General shall decree in this case as to the declaration of utility whenever it shall belong to him, according to the Law.

(Articles 115 and 117 of the Law.)

ART. 159. When works are in question which affect the general interests of the State, the declaration of public utility shall be made by the Colonial Department, or, when the power is given him by law, by the Governor-General, after following all the proceedings prescribed by the two preceding articles, and after report from the Consulting Board of Roads, Canals, and Ports concerning the proceedings sent by the Governors.

(Articles 115 and 117 of the Law.)

ART. 160. From the decisions which, in connection with public utility, the Administration may render, there shall be the right of appeal by administrative litigation, in order that, before the hierarchical superior, and after the latter has rendered a final decision, the administrative litigation shall be proceeded with, when, in the proceedings begun for this purpose, there was some error in the form of procedure infringing on the provisions which regulate the course which is to be observed.

(Article 118 of the Law.)

Approved by Royal Order of this date.

Madrid, April 26, 1883.

NUÑEZ DE ARCE.

ARTICLES OF GENERAL CONDITIONS

FOR THE

CONTRACTING FOR PUBLIC WORKS IN CUBA.

Under date of the 11th of last December the Colonial Department communicates to His Excellency, the Governor-General, the Royal Order, which says:

YOUR EXCELLENCY: Under this date His Majesty the King (whom God preserve) has seen fit to issue the following Royal Decree. Considering the reasons submitted to me by the Colonial Secretary, and in conformity with the Council of State, I decree the following:

ART. 1. The Governor-General of the Island of Cuba, as the Superior Authority representing the Government of the nation and as delegate of the Colonial Secretary, is the Chief of the service of public works of the Island.

ART. 2. The Consulting Board of Public Works is the Corporation charged with informing concerning all matters deemed convenient by the Governor-General in regard to its department and in accordance with its regulations.

ART. 3. The Inspector-General is the second Chief of the service of public works and of its personnel, and as such is charged with its immediate supervision, with sending the proper reports, with making the proposals directed to the Governor-General, and advising him on all matters on which he may be consulted. He shall take the steps and prepare the decision as to the various proceedings, in accordance with the existing laws and provisions, without prejudice to the reports which the said Superior Authority, for his better information, may in the last stage deem it convenient to demand.

ART. 4. The proceedings regarding concessions, projects, construction, and the service and preservation of public works, shall be commenced in the civil Governments of their Provinces, and must be followed in the first steps according to existing provisions, and must be continued in them, the Governor of the Province deciding, or proposing a decision, as the case may be. Only when it is a case referring to or in which two or more Provinces are concerned, or in those of general character, shall the proceedings be initiated in the General Government, which will send it to the proper authority, so that the Provincial authorities interested may be heard.

ART. 5. The Governor-General, in accord with the Consulting Board and with the Inspector-General, may decide, according to law, as to those works, the total and complete estimate of which shall not exceed 5,000 pesos, it being understood that they shall be isolated or independent works, or those relating to preservation, repairs, or additions, which will not change the form and condition of others; therefore he shall not approve projects or estimates of work, of sections of highways, roads, or buildings, the direction, project, or general disposition of which shall not have been previously approved by the Government, much less to commence work of these kinds, without express authority.

ART. 6. The Governor-General shall not give in advance any authorization, if it be not clearly within his rights or those expressly delegated to him by the Government, unless it shall be clearly within the provisions of the fifth right of the second article of the Royal Decree of June 9, 1880, concerning powers of the Governor-General; and even in these cases, in accord with the Consulting Board, the Council of Administration, and the General Inspection of Public Works, reporting by telegraph, and sending the proceedings which justify the measure by the first mail.

Art. 7. The projects and the estimates for the preservation and repair of highways, the amounts of which are already provided for by the General Budget of the Island, may be directly approved by the Governor-General, in accord with the Consulting Board and the General Inspection of Public Works; but they must be made up annually, adjusting themselves strictly to the forms and provisions previously approved by the Government, and according to the prices fixed in them as the basis of the Budgets.

Art. 8. Any change which may be deemed convenient to be made in the prices and conditions of the forms approved for the drafting of the projects and Budgets for preservation or repair, and which will essentially concern them, shall be submitted to the Superior Authority and authorized by him.

Art. 9. The Inspector-General may authorize the Chief Engineers to introduce in approved projects changes in form and detail which will not alter the conditions of resistance of the works nor their object, such as changes of levels, modification, and substitution in the kind of building, variation of some detail of construction, change in some alignment, modification of the height of the fences, culverts, and pontoons; but always providing that these changes do not increase the total estimate of the works.

Art. 10. When the said changes or the cost of the works should increase the estimates already approved, they can not be authorized by the General Inspection, which in a proper case shall submit them to the decision of the Governor-General, after an opinion of the Consulting Board of Public Works of the Island. The Governor-General shall only once authorize the increase, when it refers to a work approved by a Royal Decision, and it does not exceed 4,000 pesos, or when it belongs to a work the project of which has been approved by his authority, and the approved estimate of which shall in no case exceed 2,000 pesos; always immediately informing the Government of the authorization, and submitting the increase to its examination and approval, whenever the amount shall exceed that sum.

Art. 11. The Governor-General shall not by himself authorize any concession whatever for the construction of roads, canals, ports, works on the beaches or on the seashore, if not expressly and clearly authorized by the laws and general provisions. Such concessions shall be submitted to the general procedure indicated by the laws, and shall be decided by the Central Government, unless he has been delegated with powers for that purpose.

Art. 12. The Governor-General, after hearing the proper authorities and Corporations, shall propose whatever measures he may deem convenient for the greater activity and development of public works, as well as the modifications which he may deem necessary or advantageous, resulting from the study and application of the laws and provisions in force, for the best development of the interests of the Island.

All of which, by Royal Order, I transmit to Your Excellency for your information, inclosing a copy of the *Gaceta* in which the said Royal Decree is inserted.

And His Excellency having ordered its execution under date of the 7th instant, it is published by his order in the *Gaceta Oficial* for general information.

Habana, January 16, 1884.

The Secretary of the General Government,

M. Diaz de la Quintana.

(*Gaceta*, January 4, 1884.)

Under date of the 7th of last January, the Colonial Secretary communicates to His Excellency the Governor-General the Royal Decree, which says:

YOUR EXCELLENCY: It being just and important that the promotions for service rendered in the Colonies shall always be granted with exactness, and on the dates on which the time is fixed therefor under existing provisions, and that therefore the petition and proceedings shall be commenced and proceeded with *before* the expiration of said time, demanding that the petitions of the Engineers and Assistants of Public Works shall be made at least three or four months in advance, according to whether they serve in the Islands of Cuba and Puerto Rico or in the Philippines; dating back the promotion to the corresponding date of the termination of the period fixed, whenever the proceedings shall not have been concluded; His Majesty the King (whom God preserve) has ordered, as an explanation of the provisions of the Royal Order of September 14th, 1879, that when the regulation time shall approach for the promotion of Engineers and the Assistants of Public Works serving in the Colonies, and who desire to continue their services there, they shall send their petitions at least three months in advance, when they reside in the Islands of Cuba and Puerto Rico, and four months if in the Philippines, so that they may decide concerning them at the proper time. By Royal Order, I communicate it to you for your information and consequent action.

And His Excellency having ordered its execution on the 8th instant, it is published by his order in the *Gaceta* for general information.

Habana, February 15, 1884.

The Secretary of the General Government,

MARIANO ARREDONDO.

(*Gaceta*, February 23, 1884.)

––––––

Under date of the 18th of last October, and under number 1545, the Colonial Secretary communicates to His Excellency the Governor-General the Royal Order, which says:

YOUR EXCELLENCY: Considering the communications of Your Excellency, numbered 1454 and 1474 of the 3d and the 5th of last July, respectively, in which Your Excellency informs me of the provisions adopted for the proceedings in matters of Public Works in that Island, and of the personnel of the same—Whereas, when the Royal Decree of May 29th of this year was promulgated, suppressing the post of Inspector of Public Works for reasons of economy, it was not the intention of His Majesty's Government to alter the existing organization in the service of Public Works of that Island, as can be proved by no resolution having been taken in the matter, and the Royal Order of the 11th of the following June, in which it was commanded that the Chief of the Province of Habana should take charge of the matters entrusted to the Inspection—Whereas, the Chief of the service to whom shall be entrusted the dispatch of the matters of the Inspection shall exercise *de facto* the duties which the Royal Decree of the 11th of last December and the other provisions in force in this connection assign to the Inspector-General of Public Works; duties which, according to the Regulations, belong to the Senior Engineer of the Corps of Roads of the Island, who is at present the Chief Engineer of the Department of Public Works of the Office of the Secretary of the General Government. Whereas, this last position is of an inferior class to that which he now occupies, and besides is incompatible with the duties pertaining to the one in charge of the Inspection of Public Works; His Majesty, the King (whom God preserve), has seen fit to decree:

First. That the organization of the service of public works of that Island, as prescribed by the Royal Decree of the 11th of last December, and the other existing provisions concerning the matter, be declared in force, leaving without effect those issued by that General Government, and of which Your Excellency informs me in his communication of the 5th of last July.

Second. That the Chief Engineer of the first class of Roads, Canals, and Ports, José Paz Peraza, be appointed Inspector of the Railways of the West, giving him charge at the same time of the dispatch of matters of the General Inspection of Public Works of the Island.

Third. That the Chief Engineer of the second class of Roads, Canals, and Ports, José Pujols y Rusell, be appointed Chief of the Department of Public Works of the office of the Secretary of that General Government. I communicate it to Your Excellency by Royal Order, for your information and consequent action.

And His Excellency having ordered its execution on the 8th of this month, I publish it by his order in this way for general information, letting it be known at the same time that, as a result of the Sovereign decision, the Chiefs of this branch in the provinces of the Island shall cease to directly communicate to the Civil Governors of the same, but shall in the future do so in the same form as heretofore, to the General Inspection of Public Works, which is reestablished by the foregoing Royal Order.

Habana, November 21, 1884.

The Secretary pro tempore of the General Government,

ANTONIO DE CASTILLO.

(*Gaceta*, November 25, 1885.)

———

Under date of the 12th of August last past and number 1140, the Colonial Department communicates to His Excellency the Governor-General the following Royal Order:

YOUR EXCELLENCY: On this date His Royal Majesty the King (whom God preserve) has seen fit to issue the following Royal Decree:

ART. 1. Public works and services connected therewith which are in charge of the General Inspections in Cuba and the Philippines, and of the office of the Chief of Public Works in Puerto Rico, shall be executed, in general, by contract awarded after public bidding in accordance with existing provisions.

ART. 2. In the cases excepted from the formalities of public bidding by Article 6 of the Royal Decree of the 27th of February, 1852, extended to the Colonies by Royal Order of September 29, 1856, and by the 3d of the Instructions of August 25, 1858, issued for the Philippines, public works and services included therein shall be contracted for by private contracts or by the agreements provided for by Article 4 of said Instructions.

ART. 3. Works, parts of works, and property which shall have to be constructed or acquired in the Peninsula or in foreign countries to be transported to our Colonies, shall be excepted from the award on public bidding and may be the subject of private contract. Works included in this class, the value of which does not exceed forty thousand pesos for the Philippines and Cuba, and twenty thousand for Puerto Rico, may be contracted for by the respective Governors-General, but they must necessarily be made by the Colonial Department whenever they exceed said sums.

ART. 4. There may be executed by the system of management:

First. Works and services the value of which does not exceed a thousand pesos, but it shall not be necessary to enter into the contract for the same by means of any public bidding nor by private contract.

Second. Those exceeding said sum and included in one of the excepted cases by Article 6 of the Royal Decree of the 27th of February, 1852, and the third of the Instructions of August 25, 1858, above cited; and if it shall not have been possible to enter into a private contract for them after attempting to do so, if, from the reports of the Consulting Boards of Public Works in the Philippines, Cuba, and Puerto Rico, it appears that it is more advantageous to execute them by management than by increasing the prices or changing the conditions in order to again expose them to public bidding. In the last case an attempt shall be made to again make a contract by public biddings, or in default thereof by private contract, before ordering the execution by management.

Third. Those which, whatever may be their value, may be declared of the utmost necessity and urgency, by the procedure provided for by existing legislation.

Fourth. Those which demand especial care from a technical point of view, provided that they are proposed by the respective Consulting Boards. In the cases mentioned, Governors-General shall have the right to order the execution by the management system of the works and services in question, when the estimates do not exceed forty thousand pesos in the Philippines and Cuba and twenty thousand in Puerto Rico. When the work or service has a cost greater than the sums expressed, or should not be included in the third case of this article, its execution by management shall be referred to the Colonial Department.

ART. 5. The materials or property which are used in the work, the execution of which is ordered by the management system, may also be acquired by management. When it is considered advisable to begin the contracting of any or some of said materials or property by public bids or by private contract, it shall be thus expressly determined when the execution of the works is authorized by the proper person.

ART. 6. For the purchase of materials or property necessary for the works which shall be made by management, and for the repairs of those already constructed, the Engineers in charge of the works may dispose of an amount not exceeding five hundred pesos; and with the authorization of the Inspector-General of Public Works in Cuba and the Philippines or of the Chief Engineer of the province of Puerto Rico, when the amount exceeds this sum up to one thousand pesos. When the amount of any material or property should enter into consideration in some work of a value greater than this, its purchase or construction or extraction by management shall be authorized, and the authorization of this greater sum shall be given by the Governors-General.

ART. 7. The provisions of this decree include public works and service related thereto, whatever may be the source of the funds with which they are paid.

ART. 8. Governors-General shall make a report to the Colonial Department of the contract, by public bids or by private agreement, of all works or services the cost of which exceeds a thousand pesos, and the authorizations for the execution by management or for the purchase of materials and property which exceed said sum.

ART. 9. All the previous provisions which are changed by this decree are hereby repealed. All of which by Royal Order I communicate to Your Excellency, for your information and consequent action.

And its execution having been ordered by His Excellency, under date of the 7th instant, by his order it is published in the Gaceta for general information.

Habana, September 9, 1885.

The Secretary of the General Government,

H. R. DE REGUENGA.

(*Gaceta*, September 15, 1885.)

21634——6

Under date of August 12 last past and No. 1143, the Colonial Department communicates to His Excellency the Governor-General the following Royal Order:

YOUR EXCELLENCY: Under this date His Royal Majesty the King (whom God preserve) has deemed proper to issue the following decree:

ART. 1. The Governors-General of the Philippines, Cuba, and Puerto Rico may approve the projects of all kinds of services and public works, whether new, or of preservation, or of repair, the estimates of which do not exceed 40,000 pesos in the first-mentioned cases and 20,000 in the last, providing that their decisions are in accord with the reports of the General Inspections and of the office of the Chief of Public Works, respectively, or of the respective Consulting Boards, or with the Councils of Administration in the cases when it is proper to hear them.

ART. 2. Whenever the said resolution is not had, or when the estimates exceed said amounts, the proceedings shall be sent for the decision of the Government, sending duplicates of the documents which form the projects.

ART. 3. There shall also be sent, within thirty days, copies of the proceedings and projects which are approved in accordance with the provisions of Article 1.

ART. 4. The Governors-General of the said provinces may decide by themselves on the execution of the services and public works, the projects of which may have been approved, providing that their cost does not exceed the sums respectively established by Article 1, when there is a credit in the existing budgets for the payment of the work referred to, reporting to the Government all the decisions which shall be made, from the commencement to the termination of the work and the service, their acceptance, and the liquidations when once approved.

ART. 5. If there should be no credits sufficient in the budgets, or when the work or service should exceed the amounts referred to, the Government shall be consulted in regard to its execution, the system of management or that of contract by public bids being proposed, sending in the latter case the articles of economic conditions and the other necessary documents, and in due time report thereof shall be made, as also of the beginning and the termination of the work, sending the approval of the memoranda of acceptance and liquidation.

ART. 6. The Governors-General of the Philippines, Cuba, and Puerto Rico may advance the authorization for the approval of public works and for the construction of works destined for private service, the concession of which, according to the Law of Waters of the 3d of August, 1866, in force in the Colonies, pertains to the Government, whenever they may do so in accordance with the report of the General Inspection and of the Consulting Boards in the Philippines and Cuba, and of the office of the Chief of Public Works and the Consulting Board in Puerto Rico, and in accordance also with the reports of the respective Councils of Administration, when these should be heard, necessarily sending by the first mail the complete proceedings to the Government, which shall continue the proceedings, reserving the right to decide them finally and to grant the concession prayed for, when this shall be proper.

ART. 7. In no case may Governors-General advance the authorization referred to in the previous article, before the proceedings prescribed by the Law of Waters in force shall have been completely terminated in the respective General Government, ready to be sent by the first mail for superior decision.

ART. 8. When the resolution to which Article 5 refers is not adopted, Governors-General can not advance the authorization either to effect the use prayed for, or to undertake the projected works, being compelled to wait for the decision of the respective proceedings by the Government.

ART. 9. For the application of this decree, by public works shall be understood all those which in the Philippines and Cuba are in charge of the respective General Inspections, and of the office of the Chief of Public Works in Puerto Rico.

ART. 10. The provisions of this decree are understood without prejudice to the powers which existing legislation grants to superior Authorities of the Colonies in grave and urgent cases and in those of absolute necessity, demonstrated in the manner provided for. Their decisions in these matters shall be communicated to the Government as soon as possible for the final decision which may be proper.

ART. 11. The General Laws of Public Works of Cuba and Puerto Rico, the respective regulations for their application, that of May 21, 1868, reorganizing the service of public works in the Philippines, and the law of Waters of August 3, 1866, shall be understood to be changed in those parts which are in conflict with the provisions of this decree.

ART. 12. The Cortes shall be informed of this decree. All of which by Royal Order I communicate to Your Excellency for your information and consequent action.

And its execution having been ordered by His Excellency, under date of the 7th instant, by his order it is published for general information.

Habana, September 9, 1885.

The Secretary of the General Government,

H. R. DE REGUENGA.

(*Gaceta*, September 19, 1885.)

Under date of August 2 last past and number 873, the Colonial Department communicates to His Excellency the Governor-General the following Royal Order:

YOUR EXCELLENCY: The King (whom God preserve) and in his name the Queen Regent of the Realm, has seen fit to issue under this date the following Royal Decree: In view of the proceedings begun in the Island of Cuba, relating to the convenience referred to for the study and construction of the highroad of Victoria de las Tunas to Puerto Padre, at the first point of Manati which is shown in the second place in the plan of highroads of that Island, which was published in the Gaceta of Madrid November 23, 1883: In view of the proceedings established therein and the reports sent concerning the said highroad, as well in the Island of Cuba as by the Consulting Board of Roads, Canals, and Ports, keeping in mind the resolutions concerning said plan by the Colonial Department and by the Council of Ministers, from whose decision at appears that the highway of Victoria de las Tunas to Manatí was substituted by that of Victoria de las Tunas to Puerto Padre, and only by material error the first instead of the second was put in the second place on drafting the Royal Decree of November 23, 1883; and in view of the report which has recently been published by the Consulting Board of Roads, Canals, and Ports concerning the proceedings recently sent by the Governor-General of the Island of Cuba concerning this matter, and on the proposal of the Colonial Department; in the name of my August Son the King, Don Alfonso XIII, and as Queen Regent of the Realm, I hereby decree as follows:

ART. 1. The general plan of highroads which shall be followed in the Island of Cuba, for the purposes of Article 4 of the law ordered to be enforced by Royal Decree of June 1, 1883, includes the following:

First, from Holguin to Gibara; second, from Victoria de las Tunas to Puerto Padre; third, from Bayamo to Manzanillo; fourth, from Santa Catalina de Guaso to the port of Tánamo, through Sagna de Tánamo; fifth, from Victoria de las Tunas to Holguin; sixth, from Holguin to Jiguaní, through Cacocun; seventh, from Puerto Principe to Santa Cruz; eighth, from Santa Cruz to Sancti Spiritus, through Jíquimas, Güinia de Santo Fernandez (railroad station of Trinidad), and Banao; ninth, from De la de Guanay to Mariel, to Cabanas; tenth, from Bahia Honda to the landing place of Sabanalamar, through San Cristóbal; eleventh, from Holguin to Sabanilla (railroad station of Cuba), through Tacamaro and Mayarí; twelfth, from

Pinar del Rio to the landing place of San Cayetano, through Rio Honda and Consolación del Norte; thirteenth, from Pinar del Rio to the landing place of Bailén, through San Juan and Galafre; fourteenth, from the landing place of Bailén to those of Arroyos, through Guane and Mantua; fifteenth, from Santa Catalina de Guaso to Baracoa; sixteenth, from Cabañas to Bahía Honda, through San Diego de Núñez; seventeenth, from Cienfuegos to Trinidad, through Arimao, Gavilan, and Cabaiguán.

Highroads which are of interest to the defense of the territory: First, from Santiago de Cuba to Vicana, through El Cobre, Guisa, and Zarzal; second, from Puerto Principe to La Guanaja; third, from San Gerónimo to Vertientes; fourth, from Bahía Honda to Mantua.

Art. 2. The highroads included in each one of the two groups should be studied and constructed in the order in which they are set forth in the order.

Art. 3. The study and construction of highroads shall be suspended, the line of which shall have to follow the direction of a railroad which is in course of construction. All of which by Royal Decree I communicate to Your Excellency as a decision of the proceedings which you were pleased to send to this office, number 613, of the 22d of March, relative to the advisability of giving preference for the study and construction to the highroad from Victoria de las Tunas to Puerto Padre, to that of the first Port to Manatí of this Island, which Royal Decree should be inserted in the official Gazette of the said Island.

And its execution having been ordered by His Excellency under date of August 25 last past, by Royal Decree it is published in the *Gaceta* for general information.

Habana, September 8, 1887.

JOSÉ PUJALS.

(*Gaceta*, September 17, 1887.)

———

His Excellency the Colonial Secretary, communicates to this General Government under date of the 27th ultimo the following order number 655:

Your Excellency: The application to the projects and construction of the works which may be therein executed of the new articles of general conditions for the contracting of the same, approved by Royal Decree of the Secretary of the Interior of June 11th, 1886, and of the formulæ for the drafting of projects of highroads, in the part applicable, approved by Royal Orders of June 26th and of August 24th of the same year, in force in the Peninsula, the application of which is proposed to public works of the Philippines by the Consulting Board of Roads, Canals, and Ports, being convenient and beneficial for the better service of public works in this Island; in conformity with said proposal, the King (whom God preserve) and in his name the Queen Regent of the Kingdom, has been pleased to order that the articles of general conditions for the contracting of said works and the formulæ for the drafting of projects of highroads, approved by the Royal Orders above cited, be extended to this Island and to public works of all kinds which may be projected or constructed in the future; for which purpose there are sent to Your Excellency the annexed eight copies of said documents, destined for the Offices of Public Works of these Provinces.

And its execution being resolved upon by His Excellency under date of the 26th of last month, by his order it is published in the Gaceta for general information.

Habana, June 4, 1888.

A. DE QUINTANA.

(*Gaceta*, June 9, 1888.)

ARTICLES OF GENERAL CONDITIONS FOR THE CONTRACTING OF PUBLIC WORKS.

[Approved by Royal Decree of June 11, 1886; extended to this Island by Royal Order of April 27, 1888.]

CHAPTER I.

GENERAL PROVISIONS.

ARTICLE 1. Contractors of public works may be Spaniards or foreigners who are possessed of civil rights, in accordance with the laws of their respective nationality, and partnerships and companies legally constituted or recognized in Spain. There are excepted—

First. Those who have been criminally prosecuted, if any of them shall have been condemned to prison;

Second. Those who have failed in business, either by suspending payments or having their property attached; and

Third. Those who are shown to be debtors to the public funds in the capacity of taxpayers.

ART. 2. The person to whom the execution of a work or service for the same has been awarded, shall deposit, as a guaranty, the amount prescribed by the articles of particular conditions which may have served as the basis for the award. This deposit shall be made in the place and within the time designated by the said articles of condition.

ART. 3. The time fixed in the previous article shall not exceed thirty days, and within it there shall be presented by the person to whom the contract is awarded, the receipt which shows that he has effected the guaranty referred to in the same article. In case of failure to do so there shall, without any further proceedings, be a declaration of the invalidity of the award, and the person to whom the award was made shall forfeit the provisional deposit which may have been made in order to take part in the public bids.

ART. 4. Every contract for the execution of public works shall be made by a public instrument, which shall contain the beginning and the ending and the forms prescribed by existing legislation.

The body of the said instrument shall consist of: So much of the memorandum of bidding as refers to the proposal at the public sale, or rather the one which is declared the most advantageous; the order of award; an exact copy of the receipt referred to in the preceding article, and the addition of a clause or condition stating in absolute terms that the contractor obligates himself for the exact fulfillment of the contract, in conformity with the provisions of these articles of general conditions, of the particular conditions, of the technical conditions of the project, and of the plans and estimate. Previously to the execution of the instrument, the contractor shall have signed, at the foot of said articles of particular and technical conditions and of the plans and of the estimate, his agreement thereto.

ART. 5. The contractor has the right to obtain copies, at his own cost, of the plans, estimate, and articles of conditions of the project. The engineers, if the contractor so requests, shall certify these copies after they have been compared.

ART. 6. Contractors are obligated to submit the decision of all questions arising with the Administration which might affect their contracts, to the Administrative Authorities and Tribunals in accordance with the Law of Public Works, renouncing the rights of common law, and to the privileges of domicile.

ART. 7. These articles of conditions shall control in all matters which are not modified by the particular conditions of each contract.

CHAPTER II.

EXECUTION OF THE WORK.

ART. 8. The Engineer or the person charged with the inspection and supervision of the works shall go over on the ground, in the presence of the contractor, the line and survey of the same made before the public bidding or award, drawing a duplicate memorandum, which shall be signed by the Engineer and the contractor, showing that the survey is made in accordance with the approved project. This shall be accompanied with the plans and longitudinal and transverse profiles which may be judged necessary, in accordance with the character and circumstances of the land and of the work, also signed by the Engineer and by the contractor. One of these copies of the memorandum shall be annexed to the contract records and the other shall be delivered to the contractor, sending a copy thereof to the General Direction.

In case differences arise between the project and the comparison with the survey, the memorandum shall set them forth, and they shall also be noted on the plans and the proper profiles; all proceedings being suspended until the decision by the superior Authority, to whose knowledge the matter shall immediately be brought.

The expenses of the comparison of the general survey, as well as the making of partial comparisons on the ground demanded in the course of the work, shall be at the expense of the contractor.

ART. 9. The acquisition of lands occupied by the work is at the expense of the State; but the contractor shall be obligated to pay its value, for which he shall be reimbursed by means of certificates issued by the Chief Engineer of the province, with a credit of 1 per cent by reason of the advance of the money.

ART. 10. The contractor shall begin the work within the time set forth in the particular conditions of the contract; he shall so carry them on, that within the various times set forth therein the corresponding part shall be executed, and shall finish them within the time fixed. In the execution, so far as the results of the plans and profiles of the project or of the survey which shall have been officially authorized are concerned, the provisions of the technical conditions and of the orders or instructions given by the Engineer, or by the subordinates directly charged with the inspection, shall be followed. The contractor may demand that these instructions or orders shall always be given, and this shall always be necessary when the technical conditions or the indications of the plans are attempted to be explained, interpreted, or modified. The contractor shall have, in all cases, a right to complain of the directions given by subordinates, to the Engineer, and of those given by the latter to the Engineer in Chief, who shall decide according to their judgment of what may be deemed just and proper.

ART. 11. If in any case whatsoever, independently of the will of the contractor, the latter can not commence the works within the time fixed, or shall have to suspend them, an extension shall be granted for a time sufficient for the fulfillment of the contract.

ART. 12. From the time the works are begun until their final acceptance, the contractor, or his duly authorized representative, shall reside at a place near the works, and he can not absent himself therefrom without notifying the Engineer and leaving a substitute to give orders, make payments, continue the works, and receive the orders which may be communicated to him. When this provision is violated, all the notices which are made in the office of the Alcalde of the town of his official residence, shall be considered valid.

ART. 13. The contractor, personally or by means of his agents, shall accompany the Engineers in the visits which the latter make to the works whenever they may so demand. He shall see to it, in the same manner, that the proprietors or cultivators of the neighboring lands do not infringe with their labors on the zone devoted to the execution of the works, and that they do not deposit therein material of any kind, immediately notifying the Engineer of any infraction of these rules which may be observed.

ART. 14. The contractor can not refuse to admit the Engineers, Assistants, or Overseers in charge of the inspection of the work, nor demand that, on the part of the Administration, other experts be assigned for the inspection and measurements. If he believes himself to be prejudiced by the results of these inspections and measurements he shall proceed as indicated in Article 10, giving the reasons of his complaint and the grounds therefor to the Chief Engineer, who shall either himself decide or report to the Government; but in neither case shall the progress of the works be interrupted or disturbed for this reason.

ART. 15. The number of laborers for the auxiliary measures necessary for the execution of the works shall always be in proportion to the extent and nature of those which have to be executed; and in order that the Engineer may be sure of the fulfillment of this condition, the contractor shall always give an account thereof when it is demanded.

ART. 16. The contractor shall insure the lives of the laborers against all the accidents which may result from the work or be connected therewith. Those of the General Direction shall except those which may be declared to be imputable to the injured laborer by reason of his ignorance, negligence, or temerity.

The contractor shall make the insurance referred to in the preceding condition in the manner in which he may deem it convenient and under his responsibility, on the basis that, in case of the permanent injury of the laborer, or of his death, the latter or his family shall receive an amount equal to the pay for 500 working days; and in case of temporary injury the contractor shall pay him for the working days until eight days after his recovery, in case he does not again admit him to his employ, and only to the day of his recovery, if he returns to his employ.

The provisions of this condition govern in case that the laborer or his family renounces any other action for the payment of damages or injuries which they may have against the contractor.

ART. 17. For the lack of respect and obedience to the Engineers and subordinates in charge of the inspection of the works, or for conduct which compromises or disturbs the progress of the work, the contractor shall be obliged to dismiss his employees and laborers when the Engineer so demands, without prejudice to complaining to the Chief Engineer, in case no justifiable reason for the order is believed to exist.

ART. 18. The contractor shall be obliged to indemnify property owners for all damage which may be caused by the execution of the works, whether by the quarrying, by the removal of the ground for the building of embankments, or the occupation of the land for the formation of supports, and in order to accommodate shops and materials; by the working of roads for their transportation, and by the other operations which may be required in the course of the execution of the work.

The contractor shall fulfill the requisites prescribed by the provisions in force concerning this matter, unless an amicable arrangement is reached with the property owners concerning the appraisal and payment of the damages which may have been caused, in which case there shall be exhibited, whenever required, the agreement which may have been entered into between them.

ART. 19. The contractors may take and use the materials found in State lands or on the commons of the towns without paying indemnity of any kind, but subject to the police regulations which may be established for this purpose by those in charge of the administration and surveillance of said lands, who must be given previous notice, always respecting and replacing existing servitudes, as well as adopting the proper measures in order not to disturb the free and safe use of said lands.

ART. 20. The contractor shall not under any pretext whatsoever construct any work other than in strict accordance with the project which may have served as the basis for the contract, otherwise he shall have no right to payment for the works executed in violation of this article, unless he proves, by presenting the written order of the Engineer, that the latter has allowed him to carry them out; in which case he shall be paid in accordance with the prices of the contract.

ART. 21. The contractor shall have permission to take material of all kinds from the places that he may deem convenient, always providing that they fulfill the conditions of the contract, are perfectly suitable for the object to which they are applied, and are employed in the works in conformity with the rules of construction.

ART. 22. Materials shall not be employed until they have been examined and accepted, in the manner and form prescribed by the Engineer.

ART. 23. When the excavations produce material which is not utilized by the contractor in the works of his contract and which can be utilized in any other work of the State, the contractor shall be obliged to pile them up at places near the place of extraction and in the manner prescribed by the Engineer, the expenses of the piling up being paid for.

ART. 24. When the materials are not of good quality, or are not well prepared, the Engineer shall order the contractor to replace them at his own cost with others conforming to the conditions. If he refuses to do so, the Engineer shall make a statement of the defects which they may have and shall send it to the contractor, who in his turn shall state the reasons existing for his refusal to agree with the orders of the Engineer, and the whole matter shall be brought to the attention of the immediate superior for the determination which may be deemed just.

If the circumstances or the condition of the work shall not permit awaiting this decision, the Engineer shall have the right to impose on the contractor the employment of the material which he shall deem best, in order to avoid the damages which might result from the stoppage of the work, the contractor having the right to indemnity for the damages which may have been caused him in case the superior Authority shall not approve the decision made by the Engineer.

ART. 25. Until the final acceptance shall take place, the contractor is alone responsible for the execution of the works which may have been contracted for, and for the defects in the same which may be noted; but he shall not be excused or have any right whatever from the fact that the Engineer or his subordinate shall have examined and gone over the work in the course of its construction. As a result, and when the Engineers notice errors or defects in the constructions, whether in the course of the execution or whether after their conclusion and before their final acceptance, they may order that the defective parts be demolished and reconstructed by the contractor at his own cost. If the contractor should not deem this decision just, or should refuse to demolish and reconstruct as ordered, proceedings similar to those set forth in the preceding article shall be observed.

ART. 26. If the Engineer should find good reasons to believe the existence of hidden errors of construction in the executed works, he may order, at any time before the final acceptance, the demolition of such as may be necessary to ascertain those which are supposedly defective. The expenses of demolition and reconstruction which may be occasioned shall be paid by the contractor, provided that the errors really existed; otherwise they shall be paid by the Administration.

ART. 27. There shall be at the cost and risk of the contractor, the scaffolds, frames, apparatus and other auxiliary means of construction, observing, nevertheless, the precautions which the Engineer may deem convenient to establish for the greater safety of the laborers.

All the auxiliary means shall remain the property of the contractor on the conclusion of the works, providing the contrary is not agreed on in the particular conditions, no claim whatsoever being founded on the inefficiency of said means, or when they shall be specified in the estimate, or when they shall have been separately stated in the estimate or estimated all together.

ART. 28. No inscription whatever may be placed on the works without the authority of the Government.

ART. 29. The Government reserves the ownership of antiquities, objects of art, and mineral substances which may be utilized for public instruction which may be found in the excavations or demolitions. The contractor shall be obliged to employ, in order to extract them, all the precautions suggested to him by the Engineer, with the right, however, to indemnity for the expense which this work may occasion him.

If in the course of the construction of the work, or in consequence thereof, there should appear on the surface running water or currents of water, they shall also be the property of the Government; but the contractor may have the right to use them in the course of construction and for consumption by the laborers during the period of his contract.

CHAPTER III.

ECONOMIC CONDITIONS.

ART. 30. The contractor shall be paid for the work actually executed in accordance with the approved project or the modifications introduced therein, or the orders which may have been communicated to him in writing, providing that the technical conditions are always carried out, in accordance with which the measurement and valuation of the various units shall be made. Consequently the amount of each kind of work provided for in the estimate shall not serve as the basis for the establishment of any kind of claim, except as expressed in article 49.

ART. 31. When the contractor shall voluntarily employ, with the authorization of the Engineer, materials of greater dimensions than those set forth by the particular conditions, he shall only have a right to payment for the work which results from the cubic measurement made in accordance with the project, applying the prices of the contract. If the dimensions should be less, and nevertheless declared admissible, the payment shall be made according to the results of the cubic measurement.

The payment shall be made by reason of the augmentation of dimensions of materials whenever the Engineer may have in writing so ordered the contractor to use them.

ART. 32. The amounts calculated for accessory works, although appearing in a single amount in the general estimate, shall not be paid except at the prices and under the conditions of the contract, in accordance with the particular projects which may have been drawn therefor, or, in default of such, in accordance with the results of the final measurements.

In the same manner the extraction of rubbish and fragments which might result during the period of guaranty shall be paid for.

ART. 33. There shall be paid absolutely, but with the reduction made on the bidding, the determined amounts set forth in the estimate for auxiliary means of the execution and for the drainage, as well as for the indemnity for loss and damage occasioned by transit, use of provisional rates, alteration of drains, and similar works which do not form an integral part of the contract.

In the same way, the determined amounts for the preservation of the earthworks and constructions, and the work done by manual labor necessary for the preservation of the bed of the highroads, shall be paid for, whenever the time during which the preservation is charged to the contractor shall be fixed in the conditions. Whenever it is reduced, a proportionate deduction shall be made, and whenever it is augmented without fault of the contractor, there shall be paid, besides, a proportionate part for the excessive time.

In cases in which all or part of the preceding amounts do not appear in the estimate, it shall be understood that the expenses occasioned by those operations shall be included in the prices of the units of work provided by the estimate.

ART. 34. The payments shall be made at the times fixed by the particular conditions of the contract, by means of warrants issued by virtue of the certificates of work given by the Engineer. The warrants, or their amounts, shall be necessarily delivered to the contractor in whose favor the award of the bid of the works has been made or to a person legally authorized by him, and never to any other person, although warrants or letters requisitorial be issued by any Authority or Court for their retention, since public funds devoted to the payment of laborers or for their security are in question and not obligations of private interest to the contractor. Only the balance which may remain after the final acceptance of the work in accordance with the conditions, and the guaranty, if it should not necessarily have to be retained for the fulfillment of the contract, shall be subject to the attachment decree by said Authorities or Courts.

ART. 35. Certificates of work shall be given at the times fixed in the articles of economic conditions of the contract, having the character of provisional documents of account, subject to the corrections and modifications which may result from the final liquidation.

In order to make these certificates the elemental process which have served as the basis of calculating the average price of each unit of work shall be applied, bearing in mind the reduction which may have been the result of the public bidding, the Engineer having the power on granting the certificates to deduct as much as 20 per cent of the amount of the valuation thus made, whenever special and justifiable circumstances which must be set forth, advise the making of this reduction.

ART. 36. The certificates shall include three-quarters of the value of the materials when they shall have been actually used in the work according to their valuation made by the Engineer, keeping in mind this payment in order to deduct it from the total amount of the works constructed with such materials.

ART. 37. Whenever drainage may be necessary which, because of the circumstances, is not at the expense of the contractor, the latter shall be obliged to pay the expenses of all kinds which may be occasioned, which shall be repaid to him by the Administration apart from the contract. For this purpose payment shall be made in the presence of a person designated by the Engineer, who shall draw the lists which, attached to the receipts, shall serve as documents proving the accounts, which shall be stamped with the approval of the Engineer.

Besides the monthly repayment of these expenses to the contractor, he shall be paid 1 per cent of their amount as interest on the money which he has advanced and remuneration for the work and labor which he may have had to perform.

ART. 38. If the Government should not make payment for the executed work within the two months following that in which the certificates were given by the Engineer, the contractor shall be paid, from the day on which said period of two months terminated, interest at the rate of 6 per cent annually on the amount of said certificates.

If two additional months have passed without the payment having been made, the contractor shall have a right to the rescission of the contract, the effects thereof being those stated in Article 54, and the corresponding limitation of the executed works and materials used shall follow. The petition for the rescission of the contract based on this delay in payments shall not be acted on unless the contractor proves that at the time of his statement he has invested in the works and in the materials furnished, the part of the estimate corresponding to the time of execution which may have been fixed by the contract, and shall prove that at the proper time he has taken the necessary steps to collect the amount of the warrants issued in his favor without having succeeded in doing so.

ART. 39. In no case may the contractor alleging delay in payments suspend the works nor reduce them to a lower scale than that which proportionately is proper according to the time at which they are to be finished. When this happens, the Administration may carry out the provisions of Articles 55 and 56.

ART. 40. The contractor shall have no right to indemnity by reason of losses, damages, or injuries occasioned to the works, except in cases of force majeure. For the purposes of this article, the following only shall be considered as such:

First. Destruction by fire caused by electricity in the atmosphere.

Second. Damages produced by earthquakes.

Third. Those resulting from the movements of the land on which the works are constructed; and,

Fourth. Destruction occasioned by violence with armed hand in times of war, public sedition, or robbery by mobs.

In order to claim and obtain in a proper case the payment of the damages, the contractor shall follow the provisions of Articles 2, 3, 4, and 5 of the Regulations of June 17, 1868.

ART. 41. The contractor may not, under any pretext or error or omission, claim an increase in the prices fixed by the general terms accompanying the estimate.

Neither shall any claim whatsoever be admitted which is founded on statements made in the memorial concerning the works, their prices, and the other details of the project, alleging that such document is not the one which serves as the basis for the contract. The material errors which the estimate may contain, either by reason of variation in prices differing from those of the list or from error in the amounts of the work or its value, shall be corrected at any time they may be observed; but shall not be taken into account for the purposes indicated by article 49, except when a claim may have been established thereon within the period of four months, counting from the day of the award.

The material errors shall not change the proportional reduction made in the contract in connection with the amount which in the estimate has served as the basis for the same, but it shall always be fixed according to the relation between the amounts of said estimate (before the corrections) and the amount offered.

ART. 42. In no case may the contractor allege uses and customs of the country concerning the application of prices or measurement of the works when in conflict to the present articles of conditions or to the particular ones of the contract.

Chapter IV.

MODIFICATIONS OF THE PROJECT.

Art. 43. If, before the granting of the works or during their construction, the Administration should resolve to execute on its own account part of those included in the contract, or should decide to introduce into the project modifications which produce an increase or a reduction or even a suppression of amounts of work provided for in the estimate, or the substitution of one class of construction by another, provided always that they be of those included in the contract, these decisions shall be obligatory on the contractor, without the latter having any right, in case of suppression or reduction of the works, to claim any indemnity on account of the pretended benefits which he might have been able to obtain on the part of the works reduced or suppressed.

Art. 44. If, in order to carry out the modifications referred to in the preceding article, the Administration should deem it necessary to suspend the whole or a part of the works contracted for, the proper order in writing shall be sent to the contractor, and the measurement of the executed work shall be proceeded with in that part which is included in the suspension, a memorandum of the result being drawn.

Art. 45. Whenever, even when not stipulated in the particular conditions of the contract, it may be deemed convenient to employ material belonging to the State, the contractor shall only be paid the cost of the transportation and of the labor in accordance with the elemental prices; and if it should not be contained in this list, without any right to claim indemnity of any kind, unless there have already been furnished the materials contracted for. This alteration shall be considered a modification of the project for the purposes of article 49.

Art. 46. When it is deemed necessary to employ materials or to execute works which shall not appear in the estimate of the contract, their value shall be appraised at the prices assigned to other similar works or materials, if there should be any, and if not, shall be discussed by the Engineer and the contractor, and submitted to the superior Authority, if an agreement should be reached.

The new prices, agreed on in one way or another, shall be subject always to the corresponding reduction which may have been obtained on the public bidding.

When the employment of the materials or the execution of the works in question shall be proceeded with without previous approval of the superior of the prices which shall be applied to them, it shall be understood that the contractor renounces his rights and agrees with those fixed by the Administration.

When there shall be no agreement as to the fixing of these prices between the Administration and the contractor, the latter shall be relieved from the construction of the part of the work in question without right to indemnity of any kind, being paid, nevertheless, for the materials which may have been used and which may have remained unemployed by reason of the change introduced.

ART. 47. When the contract includes some works which are of such nature that, calculating by a determined amount in the estimate, no definite project can be made by measurement because of the circumstances, there shall be applied to these works the provisions determined by articles 43 and 49 concerning modifications of projects.

CHAPTER V.

CASES OF RESCISSION.

ART. 48. In case of the death of the contractor, the contract shall be considered rescinded, unless the heirs offer to carry it out under the conditions stipulated in the same. The Government may accept or refuse the offer, without giving to them any right whatever to indemnification, although there shall be the right for the State to acquire, after an appraisement, the tools, utensils, and property used for the works which may be indispensable for their completion.

ART. 49. When the modifications which are mentioned in Articles 43 and 45 alter the estimate of the contract in such a manner that the total amount shows a difference of a fifth, more or less, the contractor shall have the right to rescission and to payment for the materials which he may have on hand and which remain unused, according to the prices of the special list. In order to fix this difference all the alterations introduced into the estimate shall be added, though some be for excess and others for deficit.

The contractor shall have the same right when alterations arise on account of error in the material referred to in Article 41, provided that a claim has been based thereon within the time specified by said article, or when the difference arises between the detailed estimate of the works referred to in Article 47 and the agreed amount stated in the general estimate of the works.

When two or more of the reasons stated in this article appear, their results may be accumulated in order to serve as a foundation for the right of rescission.

ART. 50. When the works can not be begun because of reasons independent of the will of the contractor, or when the Government decides that the works, after being commenced, shall cease or be indefinitely suspended, the contractor shall have the right of rescission; in the proper case there shall follow the provisional acceptance of the executed works, and the final acceptance when the term of the guarantee shall have expired.

ART. 51. If the time specified for the execution of the works shall have arrived without the suspension referred to in Article 44 having been raised, the contractor shall have the right of rescission, and there shall immediately follow the provisional acceptance of the executed works, and the final acceptance, when the time of guaranty shall have expired. The same right is conceded when the suspension lasts more than one year, provided that the value of the work referred to shall be more than one-fourth of the total of the contract.

ART. 52. If during the execution of the works prices should rise very considerably, the contract may be rescinded on the petition of the contractor, provided that the proceedings instituted for this purpose shall prove: First, that the rise has taken place since the time when the public bids were had, not since the drafting of the project; second, that it is not owing to the execution of the works referred to in the contract, but to others which may have been subsequently undertaken, or to a general unforeseen cause; third, that it is not produced by circumstances of a temporary character, as agricultural or other similar works. A very considerable rise in prices is understood to be such as, applied to the execution of the works which remain to be executed, shall produce an amount greater than a quarter of the total amount of the contract.

ART. 53. In case that by reason of a rise in prices the contractor should claim rescission, the work shall not be suspended on that account.

After three months have elapsed and the Government shall not have decided concerning the claim, the contract shall be considered rescinded in fact, and there shall follow the liquidation of the works executed up to that time according to the prices of the same, without any increase or payment of any kind by way of indemnity for damages.

ART. 54. Whenever, for the reasons stated in Articles 38, 50, and 51, the contract is rescinded, the tools and utensils indispensable for the completion of the works, the employment of which shall have been previously authorized by the Engineer, and which the contractor does not care to retain, shall be taken by the Government after the price has been agreed upon, amicably or by experts, without increase of any kind under the pretext of benefits to be derived, or for any other reason whatsoever, it being understood that this payment shall only take place when the amount of the works completed up to the time of rescission does not reach two-thirds of the amount contracted for, when works of port or similar works are in question, or to four-fifths in case of highroads and works of similar character.

The materials collected and on the ground of the works, if they are actually received and are for application for the completion of the works, shall also be taken for account of the Administration at the prices fixed by the special list for this purpose; and if they should not be included in it, they shall be fixed after hearing both parties.

The materials which, collected under the same circumstances, shall be situated away from the works, shall also be taken from the contractor, provided that they be transported to the works within the period of one ·month, unless the Administration prefers to receive them at the place in which they happen to be.

The contractor shall also be given an indemnity, determined by the Government after hearing the Council of State, which shall never exceed 3 per cent of the value of the works which remain to be executed.

ART. 55. In the special technical conditions of each contract the development of the works shall be fixed, reasonable times being stated for the progress of the works during the course of the entire construction of the same.

These times shall be obligatory on the contractor, and if there should be reason for believing that within any one of them the corresponding development of the works can not take place, the expert Director shall give due notice in writing to the contractor, also making such rulings as shall be conducive to the punctual fulfillment of the contract.

If, in spite of this, the time fixed shall have elapsed, and the contractor shall not have constructed the corresponding work, the contract shall be rescinded.

ART. 56. In the case prescribed in the previous article, and when once the rescission of the contract has been decided on, it is understood that the guaranty is forfeited and that the contractor shall not have any claim whatsoever nor any other right than to the payment of the works constructed and accepted.

Only when the retardation of the works shall be shown to have been produced by unavoidable causes, and when the agreement is offered to be carried out on the extension of the time which may be designated may the Administration, if it deems it convenient, conceed such extension as may appear reasonable.

ART. 57. When the rescission of a contract takes place because of one of the reasons stated in Articles 49, 52, and 53, the contractor shall have no right to claim an indemnity of any kind nor to require the Administration to purchase the utensils and tools used for the works.

CHAPTER VI.

MEASUREMENT, ACCEPTANCE OF THE WORKS, AND FINAL LIQUIDATION.

ART. 58. The partial measurements shall be made at the times fixed in the articles of economic conditions of the contract, after citing the contractor, if the latter should desire to be present. As provisional documents they shall be subject to the corrections which may result from the final measurement, for which purpose approval or acceptance of the works referred shall not be presumed.

ART. 59. On the completion of the works their provisional acceptance by the Engineer, whom the General Direction may designate, shall immediately take place, and with the necessary presence of the con-

21634——7

tractor or his duly authorized representative. If after being expressly required to appear, the contractor should not be present or should renounce this right in writing, agreeing beforehand with the result of the operation, the Chief Engineer of the province shall ask the Governor to make a new demand on the contractor, and if he should again be absent, said Authority shall appoint at the cost of the contractor an official representative.

The result of the acceptance shall be stated in the form of a memorandum, signed by all those present, and shall be sent to the General Direction.

If the works should be found to be in good state and in accordance with the conditions, they shall be provisionally accepted, and turned over to public use, the period of the guaranty beginning to run, as also that of the preservation fixed in the particular conditions at the cost of the contractor.

ART. 60. When the works have been provisionally accepted, there shall immediately follow the general and definite measurement, with the necessary presence of the contractor or his representative named by him or officially, as provided in the previous article.

The plans and profiles of the survey shall serve as the basis of the measurement of the plottings, which shall be drawn with the measurements taken from the work and also the form and disposition in which the superficial part of the ground shall remain, in order to deduct the number of cubic meters of cuts and embankments which the contractor has executed.

All works of construction shall be measured where they shall be visible, and in places where they are not visible the dimensions designated in the plans and profiles which shall necessarily have been made in the course of construction shall be adopted, and they shall be signed by the Engineer and by the contractor.

The volume of the foundation shall be determined by means of a shaft opened at the place designated by the Engineer.

Accessory works shall be measured in a manner similar to that employed in the measurement of the principal part of the works.

ART. 61. The valuation of the works executed by the contractor shall be made, applying to the result of the general measurement and of the cubic measurements the prices which for each unit of the work are provided for in the estimate, and further keeping in mind the provisions of Articles 30, 31, 32, and 33 of these conditions. The total amount shall be increased by such a per cent of the estimate of the contract, and the reduction made on the bidding shall be applied proportionally; from the result the amount paid on certificate shall be deducted.

The liquidation shall be drawn in accordance with the formulæ and instructions in force; and, with all the facts and copies of plans and profiles, shall be sent to the contractor with permission to retain the same for a period of thirty days, in order that he may examine them and return them with his agreement or his observations.

If because of the importance of the work, or because of the kind or number of the documents, the contractor should not deem that time sufficient for examination, he shall so state, suggesting the time that is necessary, and the Chief Engineer, if there should not be any inconvenience, shall decide whether the extension of time shall be granted or not, and also its duration.

When the time or the extension has expired and the contractor shall not have made his observations, it will be presumed that he agrees with the liquidation, which in such case, as also in the case where he replies, shall be sent, with the report of the Chief Engineer, to the General Direction for the decision which may be proper.

ART. 62. During the period of guaranty the contractor shall take care of the preservation and the policing of the works, employing in them the materials in accordance with the instructions given by the Engineer. If the preservation should be neglected, and if the order of the Engineer should be disobeyed, resulting in the imperilment of transit or public use of the work, the necessary works to avoid the damage shall be carried out by the Administration at the cost of the contractor.

ART. 63. When the period of guaranty has terminated, the final acceptance of the work shall follow, in accordance with the formalities specified in Article 59 for provisional acceptance, and if the works shall appear in a perfect state of preservation, receipts therefor shall be given and the contractor shall be relieved from all responsibility.

If the works should not be in good condition, this shall be made to appear in the memorandum; the Chief Engineer shall give the contractor precise and detailed instructions to remedy the defects which may have been observed, and shall fix the time within which to do so, making a new inspection of the works on the termination thereof and an acceptance of the works. If the contractor should not fulfill these orders. the contract shall be declared rescinded, with the forfeiture of the guaranty.

ART. 64. When the final acceptance has been made, the liquidation of the executed works and the labor performed during the time of the guaranty, shall be made, in accordance with the provisions of the estimate, of the particular conditions of the contract, and of the second paragraph of article 33 of the present conditions.

ART. 65. When the final liquidation has been approved, the guaranty shall be returned to the contractor, after he shall have shown by means of certificates of the Alcaldes of the municipal districts within which the works may have been executed, that there does not exist against him any claim whatever for loss or damages for which he may be responsible, or for debts to workmen, or for materials, and for the insurance of the laborers, and also show payment of the industrial tax corresponding to his contract.

ART. 66. If the Government shall believe it to be convenient to make partial acceptances, a contractor shall not for this reason have the right to ask that there be returned to him a proportional part of the guaranty, although he shall be free from all responsibility in connection with the works accepted; but the guaranty shall remain intact until the completion of all the works, in order that it may be responsible for the fulfillment of the contract, as is provided for by the preceding article.

Madrid, June 11, 1886.

Approved by His Majesty.

EUGENIO MONTERO RIOS.

And by order of His Excellency, the Governor-General, it is published in the Gaceta for general information.

Habana, March 23, 1889.

PEDRO A. TORRES.

(Gaceta, 2d of April, 1889.)

Under date of the 30th of last April and number 534, the Colonial Secretary communicates to His Excellency the Governor-General the following Royal Order:

YOUR EXCELLENCY: It being convenient to regulate the proceedings commenced in the Island regarding works of ports and wharves and concessions of public works and to fix the basis to which this class of conditions must be adjusted, considering that the legislation in force in that Island as to that matter is the Law of Waters of the 3d of August, 1886, which is partly in conflict with the General Law of Public Works in force in the said Island, which law is with certain changes the one in force in the Island, and it being convenient not only to harmonize the first with the second, but also to make the legislation as to public works of that Antille as similar as possible to the legislation of the Peninsula, the King (whom God pre-preserve), and in his name the Queen Regent of the Realm, has seen fit to decree that Your Excellency be advised to order the General Inspection of Public Works of that Island to study and propose in the shortest time possible, and within a period which must not exceed four months, the changes to be made in the laws as to Waters and Ports of the Peninsula of the 13th of June, 1879, and 7th of May, 1880, so that they may be applicable to the Island; and the instructions for the proceedings of concessions of Public Waters and concessions to individuals of works of Ports of the 14th of June, 1883, and 20th of August of the said year; trying to make said changes be the least possible in number, and justifying the reasons upon which the proposers based the reports which they submitted, the said propositions being made by the Council of Administration of that Island and the Consulting Board of Public Works, sending the complete proceedings in the shortest time possible to this Department, with the report and proposal of that General Government, an extract of which decision shall be published in the Gaceta of Madrid, and in full in the Gaceta of Habana.

By Royal Order I communicate it to Your Excellency for your information and consequent action.

And His Excellency having ordered its execution on the 25th of the present month, it is published by his order for general information.

Habana, May 31, 1889.

PEDRO A. TORRES.

(*Gaceta,* June 11, 1889.)

Under date of the 18th of last June and No. 730, the Colonial Department communicates to His Excellency the Governor-General the following Royal Order:

YOUR EXCELLENCY: In view of the proceedings which Your Excellency has sent me with your communication, No. 1076, of the 14th of last May, in regard to the

State taking possession of the highway from Habana to Güines and to Bejucal, to which the said proceedings referred, the taking possession of which Your Excellency has ordered temporarily in accord with the report of the Consulting Board and the General Inspection of Public Works of that Island. Considering that from the same proceedings and the circumstances of the case it results that the proposal of that General Government is convenient and justifiable, as well as the measure adopted by the said General Government, the King (whom God preserve), and in his name the Queen Regent of the Realm, has seen fit to order: That the taking possession by the State of the section of highway from Habana to Güines included between the corner at Toyo and Blanquizal, and the section from Havana to Bejucal included between the station of the City Railway and the outskirts of the ward of La Víbora, which sections of highways are to-day in charge of the Municipal Council of Habana, and that the resolution adopted by Your Excellency be approved, ordering therefore the taking possession of, publishing this resolution in extract in the Gaceta of Madrid and in full in that of Habana.

And its execution being ordered by His Excellency under date of the 5th instant, by his order it is published in the Gaceta for general information.

Habana, July 12, 1889.

PEDRO A. TORRES.

(*Gaceta*, July 23, 1889.)

———

Under date of the 12th of last month, and No. 483, the Colonial Department communicates to His Excellency the Governor-General the following Royal Order:

YOUR EXCELLENCY: In view of the communication of Your Excellency, No. 450, of the 7th of last March, and the proceedings which accompany it, relative to the request of the Municipal Council of Guanajay of this Island, which asks that the State take possession of the crossroads of the highroads from Habana to San Cristóbal and from Guanajay to Mariel, which run through several streets of said town; in view of the favorable reports rendered in connection therewith by the General Inspection and the Consulting Board of Public Works, and by the Council of Administration of this Island, keeping in mind the reasons given in support of said request, and that the granting of the same will result beneficially for the general interests of the country, the King (who God preserve) and in his name the Queen Regent of the Realm, has seen fit to order: That the request of Guanajay be granted, the State taking charge of the crossroads of the highroads from Habana to San Cristóbal and from Guanajay to Mariel, and keeping in its charge in the future the repairs and preservation of said crossings. All of which, by Royal Order, I communicate to Your Excellency for your information and consequent action; and an extract of this decision should be published in the Gaceta of Madrid and in full in that of Habana.

And its execution having been decreed by His Excellency on the 4th instant, by his order it is published in the Gaceta, for general information.

Habana, June 10, 1890.

RICARDO DE CUBELLS.

(*Gaceta*, June 14, 1890.)